JESUS BEGAN TO PREACH

Raniero Cantalamessa, O.F.M. Cap.

JESUS BEGAN TO PREACH

The Mystery of God's Word

Translated by Vera Castelli Theisen

LITURGICAL PRESS
Collegeville, Minnesota

www.litpress.org

Library of Congress Cataloging-in-Publication Data

Cantalamessa, Raniero.
    [Tua parola mi fa vivere. English]
    Jesus began to preach : the mystery of God's word / Raniero Cantalamessa ;
translated by Vera Castelli Theisen.
        p.   cm.
    "Translated from the Italian La tua parola mi fa vivere, Ancora Editrice,
2008. An earlier version of this book was published in English under the
title The Mystery of God's Word (Liturgical Press, 1994)."—T.p. verso.
    Includes bibliographical references.
    ISBN 978-0-8146-3304-5 — ISBN 978-0-8146-3924-5 (e-book)
    1. Jesus Christ—Preaching.   2. Bible. N.T.—Criticism, interpretation,
etc.   3. Catholic Church—Liturgy—Theology.   I. Cantalamessa, Raniero.
Mistero della parola di Dio. English.   II. Title.

BT590.P7C3613   2010
232.9'54—dc22   2010000368

Contents

Preface

"Your word is a lamp for my feet, / a light for my path," says Psalm 119. It then proceeds for 176 verses to celebrate with great richness of synonyms the beauty of God's word. Commenting on this very psalm, Saint Ambrose affirms that "the word of God is the vital substance of our soul: it nourishes, it feeds and directs it. There is nothing that can make the human soul thrive except the very word of God." Moses brings to light the same close relationship between the word of God and life when he says to the people, "This word is our life" (Deut 32:47), and Jesus when he answers the tempter, "One does not live by bread alone, / but by every word that comes from the mouth of God" (Matt 4:4).

This book attempts to capture this grand idea of a word that becomes Life. The constant focus is to show how the word of God illuminates and engages our existence, not only human existence in general with its usual problems, but also life and the challenges that we're called upon today to face in the Church and in society.

The book was originally published in the year dedicated, by the Catholic Church, to the word of God and wished to be a modest contribution to the bishops' synod that took place on the same topic. It picks up, in part, the reflections published a few years ago with the title *The Mystery of God's Word*, enlarging their scope with the meditations held in the Pontifical Household, in the presence of Benedict XVI, during the Lenten season of 2008.

Chapter I

"In the Beginning Was the Word"

Word of God and Words of Men

1. The Word or the Silence?

There have been many attempts to change the solemn affirmation that begins the gospel of John: "In the beginning was the Word." In antiquity, the Gnostics suggested a variant: "In the beginning was Silence"; and Goethe makes Faust, his character, say, "In the beginning was action." It's interesting to see how the writer arrives at this conclusion. I cannot, says Faust, give such a high value to "the Word"; maybe I have to understand "the meaning"; but can the meaning be that which directs and creates everything? Then shall one have to say: "In the beginning was power"? No, a sudden clear illumination suggests the answer: "In the beginning was action."[1]

But are these attempts at corrections really necessary and justified? The Word, or Logos of John, contains all the meanings that Goethe attributes to the other words. One sees it in the rest of the Prologue; the Word is light, it is life and creative force. It is "an operative word," as in "the LORD commanded and they were created" (Ps 148:5). In speaking, God creates. The difference between a speculative or theoretic sentence (for example: "man is a rational animal") and an operative or practical one (for example: *fiat lux*, "let there be light") is that the first considers the thing as already existing, while the second makes it exist, brings it into being.

It is true, then, that in the beginning there was Silence, if by silence is meant the absence of every voice and words of

1

creatures. It is false if by silence is meant the absence of the word of God. It is of this silence of things, not of a primordial silence that the text of Wisdom speaks when applied to the liturgy of the birth of Christ: "For when peaceful stillness compassed everything / and the night in its swift course was half spent, / Your all-powerful word from heaven's royal throne / bounded" (Wis 18:14-15).

Christian thought has fought to give the expression "in the beginning" the true meaning intended by John. First of all, it had to free itself from the notion that the Word was uttered by the Father only at the moment of the world's creation when he pronounced the famous *Fiat lux*, "let there be light." A provisional solution in this direction consisted in distinguishing the Word as uttered (*Logos proforikos*) that begins to exist at the moment of creation, from the Word as far as it resides implicit in God (*Logos endiathetos*) existing from all eternity. The final solution, however, only came with the Council of Nicea, when the early fathers rejected the idea that "there was a time in which the Word was not." Even as "uttered Word," the Son of God is eternal, because from the beginning of time the Father pronounces his Word. In fact he himself, in his very being as Father, would not exist *ab eterno* if *ab eterno* would not have a Son who is Word.

The "beginning" in which John places the Word is therefore an absolute beginning, outside time. If there is a reference to the text of Genesis—"In the beginning, when God created the heavens and the earth" (Gen 1:1)—it is to be understood in the sense that in the moment when all things came into existence, the Word "was," already existed.

2. A God Who Speaks

The expression, "In the beginning was the Word," contains *in nuce* the whole future doctrine of the Trinity. It means that the biblical God is unique, but not solitary; that he is relationship, namely, communication, because there is no word that does not presuppose (in the case of God that does not bring into existence) an interlocutor, a "you." But in this first meditation it is not the word in the Trinity that I wish to address but, rather, the word of God in history, God's speaking to us.

The biblical God is a God that speaks. "The LORD, the God of gods, / has spoken and summoned the earth . . . / and will not be silent!" says the psalm (Ps 50:1-3). God himself repeats many times in the Bible: "Listen, my people, I will speak" (Ps 50:7). In this, the Bible sees the clearer difference with the idols who "have mouths but do not speak" (Ps 115:5). God has used words in order to communicate with human beings.

But what meaning are we to give to such anthropomorphic expressions as: "God said to Adam," "so speaks the Lord," "the Lord says," "oracle of the Lord," and others like these? It is evidently a different way of speaking than the human way; it's a way of speaking to the ears of the heart. God speaks as he writes! "I will place my law within them, and write it upon their hearts," says the prophet Jeremiah (Jer 31:33). He writes upon the heart and he even makes his words resonate in the heart. He even says so very clearly through the prophet Hosea, speaking of Israel as of an unfaithful spouse: "So I will allure her; / I will lead her into the desert / and *speak to her heart*" (Hos 2:16; emphasis added).

At times, an almost material and external way of speaking of God is stressed: "Then the LORD spoke to you from the midst of the fire. You heard the sound of the words, but saw no form; there was only a voice" (Deut 4:12; cf. Acts 9:7). But even in these cases there's a dramatization of an internal and spiritual event, always of a way of speaking different from the human voice.

God does not have a human mouth or breath; his mouth is that of the prophet, his breath is the Holy Spirit. "You shall be

3

my mouth," he says to his prophets, or even, "I will place my word on your lips." That is the meaning of the famous phrase, "but rather human beings moved by the holy Spirit spoke under the influence of God" (2 Pet 1:21). The spiritual tradition of the Church has coined a special expression, "interior locutions," for this manner of speaking directly to the mind and the heart.

Nevertheless, it's a true way of speaking and people receive a message that they can translate in human terms. God's way of speaking is so vivid and real that the prophet remembers precisely the place and time when a certain word "came" upon him: "In the year King Uzziah died" (Isa 6:1); "In the thirtieth year, on the fifth day of the fourth month, while I was among the exiles by the river Chebar" (Ezek 1:1); "On the first day of the sixth month" (Hag 1:1).

The word of God is so concrete that it is said it "falls" on Israel like a stone: "The Lord has sent word against Jacob, / it falls upon Israel" (Isa 9:7). And at other times, the same concreteness and materiality are expressed not with the symbol of a stone that hits but with the symbol of bread that is eaten with pleasure: "When I found your words, I devoured them" (Jer 15:16; cf. Ezek 3:1-3).

No human voice can reach human beings with the same depth of the word of God. It "penetrat[es] even between soul and spirit, joints and marrow, and [is] able to discern reflections and thoughts of the heart" (Heb 4:12). At times, "The voice of the LORD . . . / splinters the cedars of Lebanon" (Ps 29:5); at other times it resembles "a tiny whispering sound" (1 Kgs 19:12). It knows all the tonalities of human speech.

3. Created in the Image of God because Gifted with Speech

The nature of God's speech changes quite radically as we move from the initial affirmation of the Prologue, "In the be-

4

ginning was the Word" to the final assertion: "And the Word became flesh." With Christ's arrival, God speaks also with a human voice, audible not only to the soul's ears but also to the body. "What was from the beginning, / what we have heard, / what we have seen with our eyes, / what we looked upon / and touched with our hands / concerns the Word of life" (1 John 1:1).

The Word has been seen and heard! Yet what is being heard is not the word of man but the word of God because it is not nature that is speaking but a person, and the person of Christ is the same divine person as the Son of God. In him, God no longer speaks to us through an intermediary, "through the prophets," but directly in person, because Christ is "the refulgence of his glory, / the very imprint of his being" (Heb 1:3).

Here, however, we are not dwelling on the word of Christ; we will speak of it later and throughout the rest of the book. In this first chapter we want, rather, to meditate on what God's speaking means to us and how it can help us reshape how we use the great gift of speech.

God created man "in his image" because he was able to speak, to communicate and establish relationships. And precisely to make this possible, "male and female he created them" (Gen 1:27), namely, different. God, who since all eternity holds within himself a Word—his own Word—created man able to speak.

In order to be not only "in our image" but also "after our likeness" (Gen 1:26), it's not enough for man to speak; he must speak as God does, he must imitate God's way of speaking. And when God speaks, both the content and the impulse of his words evoke love. God speaks for the same reason he creates: "In order to spread his love to all creatures and make them glad with the splendor of his glory," as Eucharistic Prayer IV affirms.

From beginning to end, the Bible is but a message of the love of God for his creatures. The tone can change, from angry to the most tender, but the substance is always, and only, that of love. It has been said that if all the Bibles of the world, because of some terrible disaster, were to be destroyed and only one copy were to remain, and even this copy were to be so damaged so that only one page remained intact, and even this one page were to be so creased and ruined so that only one line were still legible, and this line were to be the one from John's first letter where it is written, "God is love," the whole Bible would be salvaged because it is fully contained in that line.

God has used the word to communicate life and truth, to teach and to console. The apostle Paul writes: "For whatever was written previously was written for our instruction, that by endurance and by the encouragement of the scriptures we might have hope" (Rom 15:4). In these times of mass communication that have expanded the use of words almost without limits, for both good and evil, we must ask ourselves the question, do we humans use words, both written and oral, to communicate life and truth or, rather, to spread death and falsify the truth?

In his play *No Exit*, Sartre presents a cruel image of what human communication can become when love is missing. Three people—a man and two women—are introduced at brief intervals in a room. There are no windows, lights are turned on to the maximum with no possibility of turning them off, there is an intense heat, and there is nothing besides a small sofa for each person. The door is closed and there is a doorbell that doesn't ring. Who are they? All three people are deceased and the place is hell. The man is a deserter who tortured his wife throughout her life, one woman is a child killer and the other is a lesbian.

There are no mirrors in the room and each character can only see him- or herself through the words and the spirit of the other, who reflects back mercilessly the ugliest images laced with personal sarcasm. When, after a while, their souls become transparent to each other and everyone's faults come to the surface and are scorned without mercy, one of the characters says to the other two, "You remember all we were told about the torture-chambers, the fire and brimstone, the 'burning marl'. Old wives' tales! There is no need for red-hot pokers: Hell is simply other people."[2] The abuse of words can transform life into hell.

In the introduction to his famous *Dictionary of Works and Their Characters*, Valentino Bompiani tells a true story. In July of 1938, an international congress of editors in which he participated took place in Berlin. War was on the horizon, and the Nazi government appeared masterful in manipulating words in the aims of propaganda. In one of the last days, Goebbels, minister of Nazi propaganda, invited the congress participants in the hall of parliament. The delegates of various countries were asked to say a word of welcome. When it came to be the turn of a Swedish editor, he rose to the podium and said these words in a very serious voice: "Lord, I must give a talk in German. I have neither a dictionary nor a grammar book, and I'm a poor man lost in the gender of words. I don't know if friendship is feminine and hate masculine or if honor, loyalty and peace are neuter. So, Lord, please take back the words and leave us our humanity. Perhaps we will be able to understand one another and to save ourselves." There was a thunderous applause, while Goebbels, who had understood the allusion, left the room. How awful to have to come to the point of asking God to take back words, since they can be impediments to understanding or even hurtful.

A Chinese emperor, when asked what would be the most effective way to make the world better, answered without hesitation: reform words! He meant to say: give back to words their true meaning. And he was right. There are words that little by little, have been emptied of their original meaning and have been given an entirely opposite meaning. The use of these words can only have lethal results. It's as if one would label a bottle of arsenic "effervescent digestive"; someone will surely be poisoned by it. Countries have set up very strict laws against those who falsify currencies, but nothing against those who falsify words.

There is no word so strongly affected by this process than the word "love." A man commits violence against a woman and then excuses himself saying he did it out of love. The expression "to make love" often stands for the most vulgar act of egoism, in which each one is thinking of his or her satisfaction, while completely ignoring the other person, reducing that person to a mere object of no value.

4. No Foul Language

Scripture gives us some suggestions on how to change our language and how to make good use of words. The golden rule is the one that Jesus himself gives us in the gospel: "Let your 'Yes' mean 'Yes,' and your 'No' mean 'No.' Anything more is from the evil one" (Matt 5:37). We're faced with a paradoxical and intentional formulation here, as in many other places in the Sermon on the Mount; it should not be taken literally, as if all language should be reduced to saying yes or no. Rather, it outlines a style in speaking, a certain sobriety that avoids multiplying words needlessly or giving them more weight than they deserve with various kinds of oaths.

Saint James says that language can "[have] great pretensions" both good and bad; it can "set a huge forest ablaze," as it is "full of deadly poison" (Jas 3:1-12). How many deaths language causes! In community or family life, negative, cutting, and ruthless words have the power to make individuals hide inside themselves, to eradicate a sense of intimacy and fraternal feeling. The more sensitive ones are literally "mortified," namely, killed by harsh words. Perhaps some of us have some such deaths on our conscience.

It is true that we should not worry about being hypocritical in reforming only language without starting from the heart that is its source (Saint James affirms that a salty source can't produce fresh water). But it is also true that one thing helps the other. We should not love only "in word or speech" (1 John 3:18), but we must love *also* with words and with speech.

This is why Saint Paul gives to Christians this golden rule for words: "No foul language should come out of your mouths, but only such as is good for needed edification, that it may impart grace to those who hear" (Eph 4:29). It's not difficult to learn to recognize bad words from good words; it's sufficient to follow, so to speak, their course in our mind, to see where they end up. Do they culminate in our glory or in the glory of God and of our neighbor, and do they serve to justify, to commiserate with and give value to my "I," or to that of one's neighbor.

A bad word is every word said without love. If the bad word comes from the lips, it must be pushed back in and withdrawn. The verses of the Italian poet Metastasio are not totally true:

> A voice escaped from one's breast
> cannot be recalled.
> You cannot hold on to the arrow,
> once it's out of its quiver.

It is possible to recall a word escaped from the mouth, or at least to limit its bad effect by asking forgiveness. In this way, little by little, we will learn to keep the bad word on the tip of the tongue until it begins to disappear, giving way to the good word. What a gift, then, for our brothers and sisters and what an improvement in the quality of life within the family and within society! A good word is the one able to capture the positive side of an action or a person and, even when it corrects, does not offend. A good word is above all that which gives hope.

5. Listen, O God!

The highest use we can make of words is to use them to enter into dialogue with God, to answer him who speaks in the Bible and continues to speak in our hearts. That is prayer. Humans are never quite so authentically themselves as when they speak with God. When we speak among ourselves, we tend to put on masks, to be silent, and partially to dissimulate our thoughts. Sometimes prudence and courtesy even require this of us. Only when we speak with God are we authentic, because we know very well that "No creature is concealed from him, but everything is naked and exposed to the eyes of him to whom we must render an account" (Heb 4:13).

God himself has suggested the words for speaking with him: the psalms and the many prayers spread throughout Scripture, including the Our Father, which is "the mother of all prayers." They have been revealed not so that we repeat them in a mechanical manner, but so that we make them our own and we model our personal and spontaneous prayers on the ones the Spirit inspired to the great prayerful characters of the Bible. Contrary to all human words, even the most sublime ones in literature, the words of the Bible are never worn with use, even if repeated every day. These are "inexhaustible" words. After many centuries of existence, the *Miserere* still serves to express feelings of repentance and the *Magnificat* feelings of joyous gratitude.

Jesus recommended practicing in our speaking with God that sobriety and "sparsity of words" required in human communication: "In praying, do not babble like the pagans, who think that they will be heard because of their many words" (Matt 6:7). The suggestion applies especially to prayers of petition because "Your Father knows what you need before you ask him" (Matt 6:8). It doesn't apply to prayers of praise, of thanks and benediction, however, where the opposite principle applies, formulated by Saint Thomas Aquinas in the sequence *Lauda Sion, Salvatorem* of the feast of Corpus Christi: "as much as you can, dare as much because (the mystery) is above all praise."

I would like to conclude by offering a touching example of this way of speaking one-on-one with God, with the utmost sincerity. It is the prayer, titled *Only Now*, found in the vest pocket of Aleksandr Zapeca, a Russian soldier, who wrote it just before the battle in which he died during World War II. It appeared for the first time in a clandestine publication in October 1972.

> Listen, Lord! Not once in my life have I spoken with you,
> but today I feel like celebrating you.
> You know, since I was a child they always told me that
>   you did not exist.
> and foolish me, I believed it.
> I have never contemplated your works,
> but tonight from the crater of a grenade, I looked
> at the sky full of stars above me
> and, fascinated by their brilliance,
> I understood all at once how terrible deceit can be.
> I don't know, Lord, if you will give me your hand
> but I'm speaking to you and you will understand. . . .
> Is it not strange that in the midst of a fearful hell
> a light appeared to me and I saw you?
> Aside from this, I have nothing to say to you.
> I am happy simply because I have known you.
> We must attack at midnight,

but I'm not afraid, you are looking over us.
There's the signal! So I must go. How good to have been
    with you.
I want to still tell you, and you know it, that the battle
    will be tough.
Perhaps even tonight I will be knocking at your door.
And even if I have not been your friend until now,
when I come, will you let me in?
But what's happening, I'm crying?
My Lord, see what's happening to me,
only now do I begin to see clearly.
Help, Lord, I'm going. . . . I will probably not return.
How strange, now I'm not afraid of death.[3]

Chapter II

"Jesus Began to Preach"

The Word of God in the Life of Christ

1. Preaching in the Life of Christ

After telling the story of the baptism of Jesus, Mark the evangelist continues his narration saying, "Jesus came to Galilee proclaiming the gospel of God: 'This is the time of fulfillment. The kingdom of God is at hand. Repent, and believe in the gospel'" (Mark 1:14-15). Matthew, for his part, writes: "From that time on, Jesus began to preach and say, 'Repent, for the kingdom of heaven is at hand'" (Matt 4:17). With these words begins the "Gospel," understood as the good news "of" Jesus—namely brought by Jesus and of which Jesus is the subject. This is quite distinct from the good news "about" Jesus as it relates to the ensuing apostolic preaching in which Jesus is the object.

Jesus' preaching is an event that occupies a specific place in time and space. It happens "in Galilee," "after John was arrested." The verb used by the evangelists, "he began to preach," underlines the fact that it is a "beginning," something new not only in the life of Christ but also in the very story of salvation. The letter to the Hebrews expresses the novelty in this way: "In times past, God spoke in partial and various ways to our ancestors through the prophets; in these last days, he spoke to us through a son" (Heb 1:1-2). A special period of salvation begins, a new *kairos* that goes on for about two and a half years (from the fall of 27 to the spring of AD 30).

13

Jesus gave great importance to this activity, to the point of claiming to have been sent by the Father and consecrated with the anointing of the Spirit "to bring glad tidings to the poor" (Luke 4:18). On one occasion in which certain people wanted to keep him from leaving, he encouraged the apostles to go, saying to them, "Let us go on to the nearby villages that I may preach there also. For this purpose have I come" (Mark 1:38).

Preaching is part of the so-called mysteries of the life of Christ, and it is as such that we approach it. The word "mystery" is intended, in this context, as an event in the life of Jesus bearing a salvific meaning and is celebrated as such in the liturgy of the Church.[1] There is no special liturgical feast to celebrate the preaching of Jesus because it is recalled in every liturgy of the Church. The "liturgy of the word" in the Mass is simply the liturgical enactment of Jesus' preaching. A document of Vatican Council II states: "[Christ] is present in his word since it is he himself who speaks when the holy scriptures are read in the Church."[2]

Just as Jesus, having preached the kingdom of God, went to Jerusalem to offer himself in sacrifice to the Father, in the liturgy, after having again proclaimed his word, he renews the offering of himself to the Father through the eucharistic action. When we say, at the end of the preface, "Blessed is he who comes in the name of the Lord. / Hosanna in the highest," we relive that moment when Jesus entered Jerusalem in order to celebrate his Easter there. The time of preaching ends and the time of the passion begins.

Therefore Jesus' preaching is a "mystery" because it not only reveals a doctrine but also explains the very mystery of the person of Christ. It's essential to understanding both what precedes, the mystery of the incarnation, and also what follows, the paschal mystery. Without the word of Christ, they would have become mute events. It was indeed a perceptive intuition of John Paul II to include among the "Mysteries of Light," he added to the Joyful, Sorrowful, and Glorious Mysteries of the rosary, the preaching of the kingdom, along with the baptism of Christ, the wedding in Cana, the transfiguration, and the institution of the Eucharist.

2. The Preaching of Christ Continues in the Church

The author of the Epistle to the Hebrews who wrote quite a while after the death of Jesus (therefore long after Jesus had stopped speaking), claims that God spoke to us in his Son "recently, in the past days." We must therefore consider the days in which he is living as part of "the days of Jesus." This is why, a bit later, quoting the words of the psalm, "Oh, that today you would hear his voice, / Harden not your hearts," he applies them to the Christians, saying, "Take care, brothers, that none of you may have an evil and unfaithful heart, so as to forsake the living God. Encourage yourselves daily while it is still 'today'" (cf. Heb 3:7-13).

God therefore speaks even today in the Church, and he speaks "in the Son." We read in *Dei Verbum*, "God, who spoke in the past, continues to converse with the spouse of his beloved Son. And the Holy Spirit, through whom the living voice of the Gospel rings out in the Church—and through her in the world—leads believers to the full truth, and makes the Word of Christ dwell in them in all its richness."[3]

The book of Revelation is the solemn inauguration of the new way of Christ's speaking "according to the Holy Spirit." The seven letters to the seven churches (Rev 2–3) begin with a self-presentation of the Risen One ("so speaks the Amen, the First and the Last, the Witness . . .") and end with the exhortation to listen to "what the Spirit says to the churches," as if the Holy Spirit had spoken rather than Jesus himself. It is abundantly clear that it is always Christ who speaks, but in his new way of being "according to the Spirit."

Saint John of the Cross writes that in giving us his Son, God said everything in one instance and has nothing more to reveal. God has become, in a certain sense, mute, having nothing more to say.[4] But let us be clear: God has become mute in the sense that he doesn't say new things after what he said in Jesus, but not in the sense that he no longer speaks at all. He constantly repeats and explains what he once said in Jesus!

But where and how can we hear this "new voice of his"? Divine revelation is closed; in a certain sense, there are no longer words coming from God. And here we discover another similarity between the Word and the Eucharist. The latter is present in the whole history of salvation: in the Old Testament, as a symbol (the paschal lamb, the sacrifice of Melchizedek, the manna), in the New Testament as event (the death and resurrection of Christ), in the Church as sacrament (the Mass).

The sacrifice of Christ ended and was concluded on the cross; therefore one could say that there are no more sacrifices of Christ; yet we know that there is still a sacrifice that is the only sacrifice of the Cross that is present and operative in the eucharistic sacrifice. The event continues in the sacrament; the story continues in the liturgy. The same thing happens for the word of Christ: it has ceased to exist as an *event*, but exists still as a *sacrament*.

In the Bible, the word of God (*dabar*), especially in the particular form it assumes in the prophets, always constitutes an event: it is a word-event, namely, a word that creates a situation, that always brings forth something new in the story. The recurring expression "the word of Jahveh came to . . ." could be translated as "the word of Jahveh took concrete form in . . ." (in Ezekiel, in Haggai, in Zechariah, etc).

These word-events continue on until John the Baptist. In Luke we read: "In the fiftieth year of the reign of Tiberius

Caesar . . . the word of God came to John, the son of Zechariah in the desert" (Luke 3:1-2). From this moment on, this formula disappears completely from the Bible and in its place another one appears: no longer "*Factum est verbum Domini*," but "*Verbum caro factum est*" (the Word has become flesh [John 1:14]). Now the event is a person! Never do we find the phrase "the word of God *came* upon Jesus" because he *is* the Word. Following the temporary realizations of the word of God in the prophets, now comes the full and definitive realization. The word of God has become the proper name of a person. We read about Christ in Revelation: "his name was called the Word of God" (Rev 19:13).

3. The Word, a Sacrament that Is Audible

There are no longer word-events, namely, uttered at a precise point in time and space and as such not to be repeated; yet there are word-sacraments. These are the words of God that "occurred" once and for all and have been gathered in the Bible, that are again "active reality" every time the Church proclaims them with faith. And the Holy Spirit, which has inspired them, continues to ignite them in the heart of those who hear them. "[H]e will take from what is mine and declare it to you" (John 16:14).

When we speak of the Word as "sacrament," we don't mean this term in the technical and narrow meaning of the "seven sacraments," but in a wider sense, namely, signaling Christ as the "primordial sacrament of the Father" and the Church as "the universal sacrament of salvation."[5] If we keep in mind the definition given by Saint Augustine of the sacrament as "a word that is visible" (*verbum visibile*),[6] by contrast we can define the word of God as "a sacrament that we can hear" (*sacramentum audibile*).

17

In every sacrament we distinguish a visible sign and the invisible reality that is grace. In themselves, the words we read in the Bible are only a material sign (like the water in baptism and the bread in the Eucharist), a group of dead syllables, or at the most, words in the human vocabulary like any other. But once faith and the clear light of the Holy Spirit intervene, with such a sign, we come mysteriously into contact with the living truth and will of God and we hear the very voice of Christ.

Bossuet writes:

> Christ's body is really not more truly present in the Blessed Sacrament we adore, than is Christ's truth in the preaching of the Gospel. In the mystery of the Eucharist, the species that you see are signs, but what is enclosed in them is the very being of Christ; in Scripture, the words that you hear are signs, but the thought that these represent is the very truth of the Son of God.[7]

The sacramentality of the word of God is revealed in the fact that at times it clearly operates beyond its objective content that can be limited and imperfect; it almost operates on its own, *ex opere operato* as we say in theology. In the words of Scripture there is some force that works beyond a human explanation, there is an obvious disproportion between the sign and the reality produced by it, which really makes us think of the active force of the sacraments.

When the prophet Elisha told Naaman the Syrian, who had gone to see him to be cured of leprosy, to wash himself seven times in the Jordan, he replied indignantly: "Are not the rivers of Damascus, the Abana, and the Pharpar, better than all the waters of Israel? Could I not wash in them and be cleansed?" (2 Kgs 5:12). Naaman was right: the rivers of Syria were surely better and richer in water; yet, by bathing in the Jordan he was cured and his body became like that of a young boy, which would not have happened had he bathed in the large rivers of his country.

Such is the word of God contained in the Scriptures. Among many peoples and even in the Church there have been and there will be more edifying books than certain books of the Bible (think, for example, of *The Imitation of Christ*), nevertheless none of those has the same effect as even the most modest of the inspired books. After the reading of the gospel of the Mass, the Church invites the celebrant to kiss the book and say: "May the words of the Gospel wipe away our sins" (*Per evangélica dicta deleántur nostra delícta*). The healing power of the word of God is confirmed in Scripture itself: "For indeed, neither herb nor application cured them, / but your all-healing word, O LORD" (Wis 16:12).

And experience confirms this. I heard a person give this testimonial in a television program in which I was participating. An alcoholic in an extreme stage of the disease could not endure more than two hours without drinking, and his family was on the edge of despair. He and his wife were invited to a gathering on the word of God where someone read a passage from Scripture. One sentence ran through him like a fiery flame and he felt healed. After that episode, every time he felt the urge to drink, he would rush to reopen that same passage in the Bible and, simply by rereading the words, felt his strength returning until he was finally cured. When he wanted to say which phrase had changed him, his voice broke down from emotion. It was the words of the Song of Songs: "More delightful is your love than wine" (Song 1:2). These simple words had produced a miracle.

A similar episode is found in the *Tales of a Russian Pilgrim*, and most famously, in the case of Saint Augustine. Reading the words of Paul in Romans 13:12-13, "Let us then throw off the works of darkness. . . . [L]et us conduct ourselves properly as in the day, not in orgies and drunkenness,"

19

Saint Augustine felt "a serene light" flash in his heart, and he understood that he was healed from his enslavement to the flesh.[8]

4. The Liturgy of the Word

Today, Jesus speaks in the most solemn and certain way in the liturgy of the word in the Mass. But in the beginnings of the Church, the liturgy of the word was detached from the eucharistic liturgy. The Acts of the Apostles relate that "Every day [the disciples] devoted themselves to meeting together in the temple." There they heard the reading of the Bible, recited the psalms and prayers together with other Jews, and did what is done in the liturgy of the word. Then they would gather apart, in their homes, to "break bread," that is, to celebrate the Eucharist (cf. Acts 2:46).

But soon this practice became impossible, because the Jewish authorities were hostile toward them and also because, by then, the Scriptures had assumed for them a new meaning, totally directed toward Christ. That is why even the hearing of Scripture moved from the temple and synagogue to the places of Christian worship, becoming the liturgy of the word that precedes the eucharistic prayer. When Saint Justin in the second century describes the eucharistic celebration, not only is the liturgy of the word an integral part of it, but side by side with the readings of the Old Testament are found what the saint called "the memories of the apostles," namely, the gospels and letters, or, in sum, the New Testament.

When heard in the liturgy, the biblical readings acquire a new and stronger meaning than when they're read in other contexts. Their purpose is not so much to have us know the Bible better, like when we read it at home or in a Bible school, but more to recognize the One who makes himself present in the breaking of the bread, to illuminate a particular aspect of the mystery that we're about to receive. And this seems to happen in an almost programmed way in the story of the two disciples on their way to Emmaus. It was in listening to the explanation of the Scriptures that the hearts of these disciples began to dissolve, freeing them to recognize him at the breaking of the bread.

One example among many is the reading of the Twenty-ninth Sunday in Ordinary Time of year B. The first reading is about the suffering servant who takes on the iniquity of the people (Isa 53:10-11); the second reading speaks of Christ the supreme priest, tried in everything like we mortals except sin; the gospel passage tells of the Son of Man who came to give his life for the redemption of many. Together these three passages highlight a fundamental aspect of the mystery that is about to be celebrated and received in the eucharistic liturgy.

In the Mass, the words and the episodes of the Bible are not only narrated but also experienced again; memory becomes reality and presence. What happened "in that time" happens "in this time," "today" (*hodie*), as the liturgy likes to say. We are not mere hearers of the word but also interlocutors and actors in it. The Word is addressed to us, there present, and we ourselves are called to take the place of the characters who are evoked.

Again, certain examples will help us to understand this. We read, in the first reading, the story of God speaking to Moses from the burning bush: in the Mass, we are facing the actual burning bush. We read of Isaiah who receives the burning coal on his lips that purifies him for his mission: we are about to receive on our lips the real burning coal, he who has come to bring fire on earth. Ezekiel is invited to eat the scroll of the prophetic oracles and we are getting ready to eat the being who is the very word made flesh.

Things become even clearer if we go from the Old Testament to the New, from the first reading to the gospel passage. The woman suffering from hemorrhage was sure to be healed if she could touch the hem of Jesus' garment. What about us who are going to touch much more than the edge of his cloak? In the gospel I was listening once to the episode of Zaccheus and became struck by his "modern relevance." I was Zaccheus, the words were addressed to me: "Today I must come to your house"; and one could say of me: "He has gone to stay with a sinner"; and it was to me, after having received communion, that Jesus was saying, "Today salvation has entered this house."

The same is true for every gospel story. How can we not identify in the Mass with Simon, who holds baby Jesus tight in his arms, with Thomas who touches his wounds? During one Friday of Lent, we read in the gospel the parable of the murderous workers in the vineyard (Matt 21:33-45): "Finally, he sent his son to them, / thinking, 'They will respect my son.'" I remember the effect these words had on me as I was hearing them rather absentmindedly in the Mass. I was about to receive this very Son in communion: was I prepared to receive him with the respect that the heavenly Father expected of me?

Not only the facts but also the words of the gospel heard in the Mass acquire a new and more powerful meaning. One summer day, I was celebrating Mass in a small, cloistered monastery. The gospel passage was Matthew 12. I will never forget the impact the words of Jesus had on me: "[T]here is something greater than Jonah here. . . . and there is something greater than Solomon here." It was as if I was hearing them for the first time. I understood that those words "now" and "here" truly meant now and here, namely, in that very moment and place, not only in the time that Jesus was on earth, many centuries ago. Since that summer day, those words have become dear and familiar to me in a new way. Often during the Mass, at the moment when I genuflect and rise after the consecration, I want to repeat within me the words, "Now here, there is more than Jonah, here there is more than Solomon!"

Origen said to the Christians of his time:

> You who are accustomed to taking part in the divine mysteries, you know, when you receive the body of the Lord, how to protect it with all caution and veneration, lest any small part of it, lest any of the consecrated gift be lost. For you believe, and correctly, that you are answerable if anything falls from there by neglect. But if you're so careful to preserve his body—and rightly so—how do you think there is less guile to have neglected God's Word than to have neglected his body?[9]

Among the many words of God that we hear every day in the Mass or in the Liturgy of the Hours, there is nearly always one that's directed especially to us. On its own it can fill our whole day and illuminate our prayer. But it's important not to let it fall in the void. Various sculptures and bas-reliefs of the ancient Orient depict a scribe in the act of capturing the voice of the ruler dictating or speaking: we see him totally attentive, legs crossed, back erect, eyes wide open, ears perked. It's the posture that in Isaiah is attributed to the Servant of the Lord: "Morning after morning / he opens my ear that I may hear" (Isa 50:4). We should do the same when the word of God is proclaimed.

Let us therefore welcome—as if directed to us—the exhortation we read in the prologue of the Rule of Saint Benedict: "Let us open our eyes to the deifying light, let us hear with attentive ears the warning which the divine voice cries daily to us, 'Today if you hear his voice, harden not your hearts.' And again, 'He who has ears to hear, let him hear what the Spirit says to the churches.'"[10]

Chapter III

"We Preach Christ Jesus the Lord"

The Word of God in the Mission of the Church

1. From the Jesus Who Preaches to Jesus Who Is Preached About

In the Second Letter to the Corinthians—which is *par excellence* the letter devoted to the ministry of preaching— Saint Paul writes these programmatic words: "For we do not preach ourselves but Jesus Christ as Lord" (2 Cor 4:5). In a previous letter to the faithful in Corinth he had written: "[B]ut we proclaim Christ crucified" (1 Cor 1:23). When the Apostle wants to encompass in a single word the essence of Christian preaching, this word is always the person of Jesus Christ!

In these affirmations, Jesus is no longer seen—as occurred in the gospels—in his attributes of announcer, but rather in those of the one who is announced. In a similar way we see the expression "gospel of Jesus Christ" or "gospel of God" take on a new meaning; from "joyous announcement made by Jesus" (Jesus is the subject), we shift to the meaning of "joyous announcement about Jesus" or regarding Jesus (Jesus is the object).

This is the meaning that the word "gospel" has in the solemn beginning of the Epistle to the Romans: "Paul, a slave of Christ Jesus, called to be an apostle and set apart for the gospel of God, which he promised previously . . . in the holy scriptures, the gospel about his Son, descended from David according to the flesh, but established as Son of God in power according to the spirit of holiness through resurrection from the dead, Jesus Christ our Lord" (Rom 1:1-4).

Having spoken of the Jesus "who preaches," let's now speak of the Jesus who "is preached about" by the Church. From the word of God *received* by the Church once and for all in history and always renewed in the liturgy, thanks to the Spirit, we pass to the word of God *transmitted* by the Church.

The First Letter of Peter defines the apostles as "those who preached the good news to you [through] the holy Spirit" (1 Pet 1:12). In this definition we see expressed the two basic factors of the Christian announcement. The "good news"—understood as the preaching "about" Jesus, of which Jesus is the object—indicates the *content* of the proclamation, whereas "in the holy Spirit" indicates the *method*, namely, the manner and the means with which it should be announced.

2. The "Third Search"

Let's start with the content. The questions I ask myself are very specific and timely: if the person of Jesus is the central content of the Christian message, how can we announce Christ in today's world? Which problems and new challenges does the Church's preaching need to face? Who do today's people say the Son of God is?

Let us take a hint from the solemn beginning of the letter to the Hebrews: "In times past, God spoke in partial and various ways to our ancestors through the prophets; in these last days, he spoke to us through a son, whom he made heir of all things and through whom he created the universe, / who is the refulgence of his glory, / the very imprint of his being, / and who sustains all things by his mighty word. / When he had accomplished purification from sins, / he took his seat at the right hand of the Majesty on high" (Heb 1:1-3).

This text constitutes a grandiose synthesis of the whole story of salvation that is made up by two consecutive moments in time: the time when God spoke through the prophets and the time when God speaks through the Son; the time in which he spoke through "the means of an interposed person" and the time in which he speaks directly or "in person." In fact, the Son is a "refulgence of his glory, / the very imprint of his being," that is to say—as will be clarified later—of the same substance as the Father.

There is both continuity and a leap in quality. It is the same God who speaks, the same revelation; what's new is that now the Revealer becomes revelation, so revelation and revealer coincide. And the best demonstration of this is the formula of introduction of the oracles: no longer "Says the Lord" but "I tell you so."

Now, in the light of the vision outlined in the text of the letter to the Hebrews, let us attempt to discern among the opinions that circulate around Jesus, outside and within the Church. In the field of historical studies on Jesus, what we're now experiencing is the "third search." The reason for this name is to distinguish it from two earlier searches: on the one hand, the "old historical research" that was dominant from the end of the seventeenth century throughout the nineteenth century with strong rationalistic and liberal overtones, and, on the other, the "new historical research" that started in the middle of the last century in reaction to Bultmann's thesis, which proclaimed that the knowledge of the historical Jesus was unattainable and practically irrelevant to the Christian faith.

How is the "third search" different from the preceding ones? First of all, in the certainty that, thanks to the sources, we can know much more of the Jesus of history than was admitted in the past. But most of all, the third search is different in its criteria for the attainment of the historical truth about Jesus. If earlier it was thought that the fundamental criteria to ascertain the authenticity of a fact or a saying of Jesus was its being in contrast with what was being done or thought in his contemporary Jewish world, now instead, the criteria is seen in the compatibility of a gospel fact with the Judaism of the time. If before the mark of authenticity of a saying or a fact was its novelty or "inexplicability" in relationship to the milieu, now, on the contrary, it is its explicability in the light of our knowledge of Judaism and of the social situation of Galilee of that time.

There are certain obvious advantages to this new approach. The continuity of revelation is rediscovered. Jesus is situated at the heart of the Jewish world, in the line of biblical prophets. It's even amusing to think that there was a time when it was believed possible to explain all of Christianity with recourse to Hellenistic influences.

The problem is that this gain has been so pushed to its limits as to become a loss. In many representatives of this third search, Jesus ends up completely dissolved in the Jewish world, with no more distinguishing qualities except a few details or particular interpretation of the Torah. He is reduced to one of the Hebrew prophets, or, as is commonly said, one of the "charismatic itinerants." Significant is the title of a famous book by J. D. Crossan: *The Historical Jesus: The Life of a Mediterranean Jewish Peasant.*

Without going to such extremes, even the most notable author—and in a certain way the initiator of the third search—E. P. Sanders is in the same league.[1] Having found continuity, we lose originality. We no longer understand why Jesus felt the need to say one day: "And blessed is the one who takes no offense at me" (Matt 11:6). Dissemination has done the rest, spreading the image of Jesus as a Jew among other Jews, who accomplished almost nothing new.

Generations of past scholars continue to be chastised for having constructed an image of Jesus according to the fashion or the tastes of the time, without realizing that the same thing is being done today. In fact, this insistence on a Jewish Jesus among Jews depends, in part at least, on the desire to make reparation for the historical wrongs committed against the people of Israel and to encourage a dialogue between Christians and Jews. As we shall shortly explore, this is an excellent aim but, given the way it is used, pursued with the wrong means. In fact, it's a pro-Jewish tendency in appearance only. Actually, the tendency is to heap upon the Jewish people an extra responsibility: that of not having recognized one of their own, whose doctrine was totally compatible with what they themselves believed.

3. Rabbi Neusner and Benedict XVI

Actually, it was a Jew, the American Rabbi Jacob Neusner, who brought to light the illusory aspect of this approach to the purpose of initiating a serious Christian-Jewish dialogue. Anyone who has read the book by Pope Benedict XVI on Jesus of Nazareth already knows a lot on the thought of this rabbi with whom he converses in one of the most fascinating chapters of the book. Allow me to summarize the highlights.

Neusner has written a book titled *A Rabbi Talks with Jesus*[2] in which he imagines being a contemporary of Jesus who goes along with the crowd following Jesus and hears the Sermon on the Mount. He explains why, despite the fascination with the teachings and the person of the man from Galilee, in the end he reluctantly understands that he cannot become his disciple and decides to remain a disciple of Moses and to follow the Torah.

Finally, all the reasons for his decision come down to one only: in order to accept what this man is saying, one has to recognize that he shares the same authority with God. He is not limited to "accomplishing," but replaces the Torah. After returning from his encounter with Jesus, there is a touching exchange of ideas between him and his teacher in the synagogue.

> He: "What did [Jesus] leave out [of the Torah]?"
> I: "Nothing."
> He: "Then what did he add?"
> I: "Himself."

It's an interesting coincidence that this is the identical answer that Saint Irenaeus gave in the second century to those who were wondering what new thing Christ had brought by coming into the world. And Irenaeus wrote: "He has brought the utmost novelty by bringing himself [*omnem novitatem attulit semetipsum afferens*]."[3]

Neusner has made clear the impossibility of making of Jesus a "normal" Jew of his time, or one who is removed from it only in certain points of secondary importance. The author has another great merit, to show the futility of any attempt to separate the Jesus of history from the Jesus of faith. He shows how critics can take away all titles from the Jesus of history, deny that he had (or had been given) when living the title of Messiah, of Lord, of Son of God. After all possible attributes are taken away, what remains in the gospel is more than sufficient to show that he didn't consider himself merely a man like any other. Just as a strand of hair, a drop of sweat or blood is enough to reconstruct the complete DNA of a person, so any saying taken at random from the gospels is enough to show the awareness that Jesus had of acting with the same authority as God.

Neusner, as a good Jew, knows the meaning of the saying, "The Son of God is master even of Sabbath" because Sabbath is the divine "institution" *par excellence*. He also knows what it means to say, "If you want to be perfect, come and follow me"; it means to substitute the old paradigm of sanctity consisting in the imitation of God ("Be holy because I, your God, am holy"), with the new paradigm consisting in the imitation of Christ. He knows that only God can suspend the application of the fourth commandment as Jesus does when he asks a person to renounce the burial of his father. In commenting on these sayings of Jesus, Neusner exclaims, "It is the Christ of faith who speaks here."[4]

In his book, the pope responds at length and, for a believer, in a convincing and illuminating way, to the difficulty Rabbi Neusner has. His answer makes me think of the one Jesus himself gave to the messengers sent by John the Baptist to ask him, "Are you the one who is to come, or should we look for another ?" In other words, Jesus has not only claimed for himself a divine authority but also given signs and guarantees to prove it: the miracles; his very own teachings (which is not limited to the Sermon on the Mount); the fulfillment of the prophecies, especially the one pronounced by Moses of a prophet similar and superior to him; and finally his death, his resurrection, and the community born out of him that brings forth the universality of the salvation announced by the prophets.

4. Jesus, the Son

Let us now focus on the beginning of the text from Hebrews 1:1-3 on the "son": "In times past, God spoke in partial and various ways to our ancestors through the prophets; in these last days, he spoke to us through a son" (Heb 1:1). This passage closely recalls the parable of the unfaithful vineyard workers. There also, God at first sends some servants, the prophets, then, "finally," he sends the son, saying, "They will respect my son" (Matt 21:33-41).

In a chapter of the book on Jesus of Nazareth, Benedict XVI shows the fundamental difference between the title of "the Son of God" and "the Son" without any other additions. The simple title of "Son," contrary to what one might think, is much more deeply relevant than that of "Son of God." The latter title was also used by the people of Israel to define their kings, as it was by the pharaohs, oriental kings, and Roman emperors. By itself, therefore, the title would not have been sufficient to distinguish the person of Christ from every other "Son of God."

But the case of the title of "Son," without anything added, is different. It appears in the gospels as exclusive of Christ and it is with this title that Jesus expresses his profound identity. After the gospels, it is actually the letter to the Hebrews that validates more strongly this absolute use of the title "the Son" that surfaces in it five times.

The most important text in which Jesus declares himself "the Son" is Matthew 11:27: "All things have been handed over to me by my Father. No one knows the Son except the Father, and no one knows the Father except the Son and anyone to whom the Son wishes to reveal him." Scholars explain that this saying has a clear Aramaic origin, and shows that the later developments we read in this regard in the Gospel of John have their distant origin in the very consciousness of Christ.

The pope remarks in his book that such a total and absolute communion of knowledge between the Father and the Son can't be explained without an ontological communion, one of being. Further formulations that culminate in the definition of Nicea of the Son as "begotten, not made, one in Being with the Father," are therefore rather bold developments, yet coherent with the gospel facts.

The strongest proof of the consciousness that Jesus had of his identity as Son is his prayer in which the filial relationship is not only declared but lived and experienced. As to the manner and frequency with which it recurs in the prayer of Christ, the exclamation "Abba" testifies to an intimacy and familiarity with God that has no equal in the traditions of Israel. If the expression has been preserved in the original language and has become the trademark of Christian prayer (see Gal 4:6; Rom 8:15) it is precisely because one was convinced that it was the typical form of the prayer of Jesus.[5]

This gospel fact sheds an unusual light on the current debate surrounding the person of Jesus. In the introduction to his book, the pope quotes the declaration of Rudolf Schnackenburg, who claims that "without being rooted in God, the person of Jesus remains fleeting, unreal and inexplicable." The pope claims, "This is the base on which my book is built: it considers Jesus from the starting point of his communion with the Father. This is the real center of his personality."[6]

In my opinion, this sheds light on the problematic aspect of historical research on Jesus that not only leaves aside but also excludes faith from the start, accepting the historical plausibility of the one who has at times been defined as "the Jesus of the atheists." I don't mean at this time to speak of the faith in Christ and of his divinity, but of faith in the most common meaning of the word, of faith in the existence in God.

I don't mean to imply at all that nonbelievers have no right to be involved with Jesus. What I wish to emphasize, starting from the quoted assertions of the pope, are the consequences that come from such a starting point, or how the "pre-understanding" of the nonbeliever weighs much more heavily on historical research than that of the believer. That is the opposite of what nonbelieving scholars think.

If one negates or puts aside faith in God, not only is divinity or the so-called Christ of faith eliminated, but the historical Jesus as well, and not even Jesus the man is salvaged. No one can historically question that the Jesus of the gospels lives and operates in constant reference to the heavenly Father, that he prays and teaches to pray, and that he bases everything on a faith in a God that "nourishes the birds of the air and clothes the lilies of the field." If one eliminates this dimension from the Jesus of the gospels, absolutely nothing remains of him.

Therefore, if we start from the presupposed, silent, or declared premise that God doesn't exist, Jesus, then, is merely one of the many deluded beings who has prayed to, adored, or spoken with its own shadow, or with the projection of its own essence, as Feuerbach would say. Jesus would be the more illustrious victim of what the militant atheist Richard Dawkins defines as "the God's delusion."[7] But how can one explain, then, that the life of this man "has changed the world," and, within a span of two thousand years, continues to engage spirits like no other? If the illusion is capable of producing what Jesus has produced throughout history, then Dawkins and others should perhaps review their idea of illusion.

There is only one way out of this difficulty, and it surfaced in the context of the Jesus Seminar at Berkeley in the United States. Jesus, some at the seminar opined, was not a Jewish believer, but an itinerant philosopher, much like the Cynics[8]; he did not preach a reign of God, nor a forthcoming end of the world; he only uttered maxims full of wisdom in the style of a Zen master. His purpose was to reawaken in humans the consciousness of self, to convince them that they didn't need him or any other god, because they had within themselves a divine spark.[9] These notions have been preached for decades by the New Age movement and comprise just one more image of Jesus as a product of the current fashion. It's true that without the sense of deep roots in God, the figure of Jesus remains "fleeting, unreal and inexplicable."

Luckily, this blind alley doesn't represent the end result of all the recent historical research on Jesus, nor its most accredited outcome. One positive result coming out of the sphere of the so-called third search is that regarding the divine cult rendered to Jesus. For almost a century, since Wilhelm Bousset in 1913 wrote his famous book on Jesus Kyrios,[10] the dominant idea in the field of critical studies was that the cult of Jesus as divine being was to be found in the Hellenistic context, long after Christ's death. Recently, the question has been revisited from the ground up by Larry Hurtado, professor of language, literature, and New Testament theology at the University of Edinburgh, and this is the conclusion he reaches at the end of his seven-hundred-page study:

> Moreover, devotion to Jesus as divine erupted suddenly and quickly, not gradually and late, among first-century circles of followers. More specifically, the origins lie in Jewish Christian circles of the earliest years. Only a certain wishful thinking continues to attribute the reverence of Jesus as divine decisively to the influence of pagan religion and the influx of Gentile converts, characterizing it as developing late and incrementally. Furthermore, devotion to Jesus as the "Lord," to whom cultic reverence and total obedience were the appropriate response, was widespread, not confined or attributable to particular circles, such as "Hellenists" or Gentile Christians of a supposed Syrian "Christ cult." Amid the diversity of earliest Christianity, belief in Jesus' divine status was amazingly common.[11]

This rigorous historical conclusion should end the opinion, still dominant in a certain kind of literature, that the divine cult of Christ would be a later outcome of faith (imposed by law by Constantine at Nicea in 325, according to Dan Brown in his *The Da Vinci Code*).

5. The Great Turning Point

Nothing in the New Testament is more useful in shedding light on the uniqueness of Christ than the comparison with John the Baptist. The theme of completion, of historical turning point that is realized in the passing from the prophets to Christ, emerges clearly from the texts in which Jesus expresses his relationship with the Precursor. Today, scholars recognize that the passages read in this regard in the gospels are not inventions or apologetic adaptations of the community subsequent to Easter, but that in their substance they go back to the historical Jesus. Some of the texts actually become inexplicable if attributed to the Christian community of a later period.[12]

The most complete text where Jesus expresses his relationship to John the Baptist is the gospel passage in which John, from prison, sends his disciples to ask Jesus, "Are you the one who is to come, or should we look for another?" (Matt 11:2-6; Luke 7:19-23).

The preaching of the Rabbi of Nazareth that he himself had baptized and presented to Israel seems to John to differ from the flamboyant one he expected. More than the imminent judgment of God, he preaches the real, immediate mercy offered to all, both just and sinners. Jesus dispels the doubts of the Precursor, making reference to the messianic signs taking place in him.

But the most relevant item of the whole passage is the praise that Jesus has for the Baptist after John's messengers have moved away: "Then why did you go out? To see a prophet? Yes, I tell you, and more than a prophet. . . . Amen, I say to you, among those born of women there has been none greater than John the Baptist; yet the least in the kingdom of heaven is greater than he. From the days of John the Baptist until now, the kingdom of heaven suffers violence, and the violent are taking it by force. All the prophets and the law prophesied up to the time of John. And if you are willing to accept it, he is Elijah, the one who is to come. Whoever has ears ought to hear" (Matt 11:9-15).

From these words, one thing seems unequivocal: between the mission of John the Baptist and that of Jesus, something so decisive has happened as to create a deep divide between the two periods. The center of gravity of history has shifted and the most important event is no longer located in a more or less imminent future, but it is "here and now," in the kingdom that is already operative in the person of Christ. Between the two preachings, a shift in quality has occurred: the smallest of the new order is superior to the greatest of the preceding order.

This theme of the completion and historic turning point is confirmed in many other contexts of the gospel. It suffices to remember certain words of Jesus such as, "[T]here is something greater than Jonah here. . . . there is something greater than Solomon here" (Matt 12:41-42); and, "But blessed are your eyes, because they see, and your ears, because they hear. Amen, I say to you, many prophets and righteous people longed to see what you see but did not see it, and to hear what you hear but did not hear it" (Matt 13:16-17). All the so-called parables of the kingdom (think for instance of the hidden treasure and the precious pearl) express the same basic idea: with Jesus, the decisive hour of history has struck and the decision on which salvation is based takes place in front of him.

This realization pushed Bultmann's disciples to separate from their master. Bultmann placed Jesus in Judaism, making him a premise of Christianity but not yet a Christian; he attributed instead the great turning point to the faith of the post-Easter community. Bornkamm and Conzelmann realized the impossibility of this thesis, saying that the "historic turning point" happens already in the preaching of Jesus. John belongs to the "premises" and to the preparation, but with Jesus we are well into the times of fulfillment.

In the theology of Luke it's obvious that Jesus occupies "the center of times." With his coming he has divided history into two parts, creating a "before" and an "after" that are absolute. Today, especially in the lay press, it's becoming common practice to abandon the traditional way of placing a date on events "before Christ" or "after Christ" (*ante Christum natum* and *post Christum natum*) in favor of a more neutral formula, "before the common era" and "of the common era." This choice is motivated by the desire not to offend people of other religions who use Christian chronology. This way must be respected, but for Christians the "discriminating" role of the coming of Christ for the religious history of humankind remains undisputed.

6. The New Prophecy of John the Baptist

John the Baptist can enlighten us on how to fulfill our obligation of announcing Christ in today's world. Jesus defines John the Baptist as "more than a prophet," but where is the prophecy in his case? The prophets announced a future salvation, but the Precursor is not one to announce a future salvation; he points to one that is present. How then can he be called a prophet? Isaiah, Jeremiah, and Ezekiel helped the people surmount the time barrier while John the Baptist helps the people to surmount the even thicker barrier of contrary appearances, of scandal, of triviality, and of poverty that accompany the fateful hour.

It is easy to believe in something grandiose and divine when projecting an indefinite future "in those days," "in the last days," in a cosmic frame of reference, the sky exuding sweetness and the earth opening up to allow the Savior to blossom

37

forth. It's more difficult when one has to say, "Here he is! It's him!" and this of a man about whom everything is known, including where he comes from, what job he exercised, who his mother was.

With the words, "[T]here is one among you whom you do not recognize" (John 1:26), John the Baptist inaugurated the new prophecy, that of the time of the Church, that doesn't consist in announcing a distant and future salvation but reveals the hidden presence of Christ in the world. In pulling the veil from the eyes of the people, it shakes their indifference, repeating with Isaiah, "See, I am doing something new! / Now it springs forth, do you not perceive it?" (cf. Isa 43:19).

It's true that now twenty centuries have passed and we know many more things about Jesus than John did. But the scandal is not removed. In the time of John, the scandal came from the *physical* body of Jesus, from his flesh so similar to ours except in sin. Even today, it is his body, his flesh that causes difficulty and scandalizes—his *mystical* body, the Church, so similar to the rest of humanity, alas, not excluding even sin.

We read in Revelation: "Witness to Jesus is the spirit of prophecy" (Rev 19:10), namely, in order to give testimony to Jesus, the spirit of prophecy is required. Does this spirit of prophecy exist in the Church? Is it cultivated? Is it encouraged? Or is it thought, tacitly, that one can do without it, relying more on human means and strategies?

John the Baptist teaches us that a great doctrine and eloquence are not needed to be a prophet. He is not a great theologian, displays a rudimentary and weak Christology, and doesn't yet know the highest titles of Jesus: Son of God, the Word, or even Son of Man. Yet he is so capable of making the greatness and uniqueness of Christ felt. He uses very simple, peasant-like images, such as, "I am not worthy to loosen the ties of his sandals." In the words of John the Baptist, the world and humanity appear contained in a sieve that he, the Messiah, holds and shakes in his hands. In front of him is decided who remains and who falls, what is good grain and what is chaff that the wind disperses.

In 1992, a retreat for priests took place in Monterrey, Mexico, on the occasion of the five hundred years since the first evangelization of Latin America. Present were seventeen hundred priests and about seventy bishops. During the sermon of the last Mass, I had spoken of the urgent need of the Church for prophecy. After communion, there was the prayer for a new Pentecost among small groups scattered in the large basilica, and I remained in the presbytery. At a certain point, a young priest approached me in silence, knelt before me, and, with an expression that I will never forget, said, "Bendigame, Padre, quiero ser profeta de Dios!" (Bless me, Father, I want to be a prophet of God!) I was very moved because I could see that he was obviously driven by grace.

We could humbly make the desire of that priest our own, saying, "I want to be a prophet for God." Small, unknown by all, no matter, but one who, as Paul VI used to say, has "fire in his heart, words on his lips and prophecy in his eyes."[13]

Chapter IV

"Announcing the Gospel in the Holy Spirit"

The Holy Spirit, the Power of the Announcement

1. Dabar *and* Ruach: *Word and Spirit*

Having spoken of the basic *content* of Christian preaching, namely, of the announcement of Christ in the current cultural context, we now move on to speak of its *method*, which as Scripture states, consists essentially in announcing Christ "through the holy Spirit" (1 Pet 1:12).

If I want to spread any news, my first problem is the medium I choose, be it newspapers, radio, or television. The means are so important that the modern science of social communication has coined the slogan, "The medium is the message" (M. McLuhan).

The primeval and natural means by which words are transmitted is the breath, the puff of air, the voice. It takes the word formed in the secret of my mind and brings it to whoever is listening. All the other means simply empower and amplify this first medium. Even writing comes later and presupposes the live voice, since the letters of the alphabet are simply signs indicating sounds.

Even the word of God follows this law. Can my breath animate your word or your breath animate my word? No, just as my word can only be pronounced with my breath and your word with your breath, the word of God can only be brought to life by the very breath, the *ruach*, of God which is the Holy Spirit.

This is an extremely simple and almost obvious truth, but of the utmost importance. It is the fundamental law of every announcement and every evangelization. Human news is transmitted either by voice, radio, cable, satellite, or the like, while divine news is transmitted through the Holy Spirit, which is its true and essential means of communication. Without it, nothing is perceived of the message but its human outer layer. The words of God are "spirit and life" (cf. John 6:63) and can be transmitted and received only "in the Spirit."

This fundamental law is the one we also see enacted, concretely, in the history of salvation. Jesus began to preach "in the power of the Spirit" (Luke 4:14ff.). He himself declared, "The Spirit of the Lord is upon me, / because he has anointed me / to bring glad tidings to the poor" (Luke 4:18).

After Easter, the disciples were told by Jesus not to go away from Jerusalem until they had been invested by a power from above: "But you will receive power when the holy Spirit comes upon you, and you will be my witnesses" (Acts 1:8). The whole account of Pentecost serves to underline this truth. The Holy Spirit comes and then Peter and the other apostles begin to speak aloud of Christ crucified and risen, and their words have such power that three thousand people feel their hearts being pierced. The Holy Spirit, descended upon the apostles, is transformed within them in an irresistible impulse to evangelize.

Saint Paul even asserts that without the Holy Spirit it is impossible to proclaim that Jesus is Lord, this being the most basic tenet and the very start of every Christian announcement (cf. 1 Cor 12:3).

No one will ever be able to express better the intimate connection that exists between evangelization and the Holy

Spirit than Jesus did the very night of Easter. Appearing to the apostles in the cenacle, he said, "As the Father has sent me, so I send you." Then he breathed over them and said, "Receive the holy Spirit" (John 20:21-22). In conferring upon the apostles the mandate to go out into the world, Jesus also gave them the Spirit to accomplish the task, and gave it through the sign of the breath.

This intimate connection between word (the *dabar*) and the breath or spirit (the *ruach*) is visible from one end to the other of the Bible. They are the two great forces that together create and move the world: "By the LORD's word the heavens were made; / by the breath of his mouth all their host" (Ps 33:6); "He shall strike the ruthless with the rod of his mouth, / and with the breath of his lips he shall slay the wicked" (Isa 11:4).

The prophets are seen at the same time as men of the word and as men of the Spirit: "My spirit which is upon you / and my words that I have put into your mouth / Shall never leave your mouth" (Isa 59:21). At times it is the word of God that comes upon them and makes them prophets; at other times (as in Isa 61:1) it is the Spirit of the Lord that performs the same function.

There is a perfect reciprocity between the two realities that has its distant roots in the Trinity itself. The Spirit proceeds "through" the Son, but the Son also is generated "in" the Spirit. In the *revelation*, the Spirit gives us the word. "[H]uman beings moved by the holy Spirit spoke under the influence of God" (2 Pet 1:21). And it is this very word or Scripture, that when read with faith, reveals the Holy Spirit. In *redemption*, again, there is this circularity: at the moment of the incarnation, the Holy Spirit gives us the living word of God that is Jesus "conceived through the Holy Spirit"; in the paschal mystery it is the word made flesh that, from the cross, diffuses the Holy Spirit upon the Church.

2. The Means: Prayer

I have developed these theological reflections on the role of the Holy Spirit in the announcement hastily and succinctly because I feel more pressed to develop the second point: what to do, concretely, to attain the Holy Spirit in our evangelization, that we, too, may be invested by the power from on high, as in a "new Pentecost."

I will highlight two means that I find essential to this aim: prayer and rectitude of intention. The things I say apply to any form of service of the word and are relevant to all, even if not strictly involved in the proclamation of the good news.

Relative to preaching, it's easy to know how to obtain the Holy Spirit. It suffices to see how Jesus obtained it and how the Church did so on the day of Pentecost. Luke describes the event of the baptism of Jesus thusly: "Jesus also had been baptized and was praying, heaven was opened and the holy Spirit descended upon him in bodily form like a dove" (Luke 3:21-22). "While he was in prayer," one could say that for Saint Luke it was the prayer of Jesus that tore open the heavens and allowed the Holy Spirit to descend.

A little further, in the same Gospel of Luke, we read that "great crowds assembled to listen to him and to be cured of their ailments, but he would withdraw to deserted places to pray" (Luke 5:15-16). That opposing "but" is very eloquent. It creates a contrast between the crowds pressing in and the decision of Jesus not to let himself be trampled by the crowd and bereft of his dialogue with the Father.

If we now pass from Jesus to the Church, we notice the same thing. At Pentecost, the Holy Spirit descended upon the apostles while they "devoted themselves with one accord to prayer" (Acts 1:14). The only thing we can do in relationship to the Holy Spirit, the only power we have over it, is to invoke it and to pray; there are no other ways. But this "weak" means of prayer and invocation is, in reality, infallible, as Luke sees it: "[H]ow much more will the Father in heaven give the holy Spirit to those who ask him?" (Luke 11:13). God has committed himself to giving the Holy Spirit to whoever prays.

Next to personal prayer, there is also communal prayer. The word of God loves to come to the announcer while in prayer with a community. There is no gift more precious for an announcer or pastor of souls than to be surrounded by a group of people with whom to pray in all simplicity, like a brother among brothers with no distinction of level or hierarchy. So were the apostles with women and disciples in the cenacle before going out onto the streets of Jerusalem. Later, when they are in front of the people, the apostles once again don their apostle cloaks and assume their authority.

In chapter 4 of Acts, we see how the community in prayer, with the strength of the charisma manifested in it, imparts courage to the apostles Peter and John, who, threatened by the Sanhedrin and uncertain as to what to do, return to announcing Christ with boldness (*parrhesia*).

We are exposed to two main dangers. One is inertia or laziness, doing nothing and letting others do everything. The other is throwing oneself in feverish and empty human activity, thus losing contact, little by little, with the source of the word and its efficacy. This, too, would be a step toward failure. The more evangelization and activity increase, the more prayer must grow in intensity.

One could object that this is absurd, that time is what it is. True, but is it not possible that he who multiplied the bread can also multiply time? Actually, this is what God does continually and what we experience every day. After having prayed, the same things can be done in less than half the time. Some ask how we can stay quietly in prayer and not run when the house is on fire, but imagine what would happen to a team of firefighters that would run to extinguish a fire realizing too late that they don't have even a drop of water in their tanks. We are like that when we run out to preach without praying. It's not that words fail us; on the contrary, the less we pray, the more we speak. But they are empty words that don't penetrate anyone's heart.

The process of evangelizing has a vital need for an authentic prophetic spirit. Only a prophetic kind of evangelization can shake the world. In the book of Revelation we read these words: "Witness to Jesus is the spirit of prophecy" (Rev 19:10). It's like saying, the soul of evangelization (the "witness to Jesus" is equivalent to evangelization!) is prophecy. And it is truly from prayer that this prophetic spirit is attained.

But what happens of such importance in prayer as to thereby obtain the Holy Spirit? By the mere fact of choosing to pray, we submit ourselves to God, in a posture of obedience and openness in his regard. We confess that "the power belongs to God" (Ps 61:12). God can only invest with his authority the person who accepts his will; otherwise it would be magic, not prophecy.

The apostle Peter used to say, to explain the incredulity on the part of the heads of the Sanhedrin, that God gives the Holy Spirit "to those who obey him" (cf. Acts 5:32). He gives it to the obedient ones. We have to die to ourselves, let our hearts be torn open, to completely accept the Father's will that is so much greater and different than ours. I am convinced that there were many nights of Gethsemane in the life of Jesus, not only one. There, he battled with God, not to bend God to his will, as Jacob did in his struggle with God, but to bend his own human will to God and say, face-to-face with each new difficulty and challenge, "Fiat, yes: let your will be done."

After such nights, Jesus would return to the crowds, who said, full of amazement, "He speaks with authority! From where does he get all this authority?" Of course he spoke with authority, the very authority of God, because when one submits completely to God, then, mysteriously, God surrenders to him; he confides his Spirit and power to him, knowing that he will not abuse it for himself or his own glory or to enslave his brothers and sisters. The words he pronounces pierce the heart, and he himself experiences an authority coming from a source other than his own.

3. To Speak with Humility

Besides prayer, another very important medium to allow the Holy Spirit to work through the word of the announcer is the rectitude of intention. For God, intention is virtually everything. A human being sees what is external, but God sees through the intention of the heart (cf. 1 Sam 16:7). For God, an action is as valid as the intention with which it is performed. The Holy Spirit cannot work in our evangelization if its motivation is not pure. It can't be an accomplice to lies. It cannot empower the vanity of human beings. We must ask ourselves why we want to preach and evangelize. "Why" we preach is as important as "what" we preach. Nothing dims and diminishes the power of our preaching as much as the lack of purity of intention.

I want to mention two directions in which it's especially important to work in order to purify our intentions: humility and love.

Saint Paul underscores the fact that one can announce Christ for neither good nor wholesome purposes: "Of course, some preach Christ from envy and rivalry . . . not from pure motives" (Phil 1:15-17). One can preach Christ for two basic purposes, for oneself or for Christ. This is why the Apostle declares solemnly, "For we do not preach ourselves but Jesus Christ as Lord" (2 Cor 4:5).

In the Act of the Apostles, Luke wanted to create a silent antithesis between Pentecost and Babel as a way of presenting the Church as the anti-Babel. But in what does the contrast between the two situations consist? Why are languages confused in Babel and no one understands the other, even if speaking the same language, while at Pentecost everyone understands each other, even speaking different languages? The explanation is found in the Bible itself. It is written that the builders of the tower of Babel started their work, saying, "Come, let us build for ourselves a city and a tower with its top in the sky, and so make a name for ourselves; otherwise we shall be scattered all over the earth" (Gen 11:4). Indeed, "Let us make a name for ourselves." Not, "Let us make a name for God."

At Pentecost, everyone understands the apostles because they proclaim "the mighty acts of God" (Acts 2:11) and not themselves, and they have converted in a radical way. They no longer discuss who among them is the greatest, but they are concerned only with the greatness and majesty of God; they are "inebriated" by his glory. Here lies the explanation of that mass conversion of three thousand people, why people, on hearing Peter's words, felt their hearts being pierced. The Holy Spirit passed without obstacle through his word, because the intention was "upright."

This is also the path to an authentic ecumenical understanding in evangelization. As long as we work to make a name for ourselves or our movement, our particular religious order, our church or denomination, we can only be divided and torn by the spirit of competition and rivalry, as in actual fact has happened in the past. When we're converted to the glory of God and together announce his great works in brotherly agreement, respecting the rules of everyone's church and in a spirit of humility and obedience, everyone will listen to us, and people will feel their heart being touched.

The solution is to ask God to let us have a fiery experience of his glory, as he did with certain prophets. Isaiah, seeing

47

the sanctity and glory of God, shouted, "Woe is me, I am doomed" (cf. Isa 6:5). Ezekiel fell to the ground as if dead (cf. Ezek 1:28) and God commanded, "Now go, and preach to my people!" These were new men, having died to their personal glory and therefore capable of "creating a disturbance all over the world" (Acts 17:6). The world is disarmed against such men and with them, cannot put into action its power of seduction and flattery.

The announcer has a powerful ally in the fight against vanity and self-complacency: the conscience of one's own sin and deformity in relation to the word he announces. Every time he shouts against some sin, if he listens carefully, he will hear within himself a boom of the word that is being shouted at him: "You are the man" (cf. 2 Sam 12:7). This is what Nathan did with David after his sin. And there are plentiful examples of such behavior, for instance, when the announcer explains the parable of the good Samaritan and speaks about the priest and the Levite who move on; also when he speaks of the servant who has been pardoned of a huge debt and doesn't remit the small debt to his own brethren.

One day, I was on my way to an important preaching engagement (I was going to preach my first Lent at the Papal Household), and on the train, while reciting the Liturgy of the Hours, I ran across Psalm 50 that says, "But to the wicked God says: / 'Why do you recite my commandments / and profess my covenant with your lips? / You hate discipline; / you cast my words behind you! . . . I accuse you, I lay the charge before you.'" (Ps 50:16, 21).

Before I could preach the Word to others, the Word was preaching to me. And how it was preaching! In fact, I was, without a doubt, that sinner, who always has on his lips the rules and alliance of God, but doesn't want to hear of his "discipline," thus avoiding the austerity required and fleeing the radical demands of the Word.

Saint Paul has a long speech against those (in this case, his fellow Jews) who, despite being repositories of Scripture, use it only to judge others and not themselves. He says, "Now if you call yourself a Jew and rely on the law and boast of God and know his will and are able to discern what is important . . . and if you are confident that you are a guide for the blind and a light for those in darkness, that you are a trainer of the foolish and a teacher of the simple, because in the law you have the formulation of knowledge and truth—then you who teach another, are you failing to teach yourself?" (Rom 2:17-21). The Apostle gives a few examples, but we can give others: You who condemn hate and preach love, do you really love your neighbor? Do you love your enemies? You who proclaim "Blessed are the poor in spirit," are you really detached from things, from rewards? Are you ready to leave everything? Are you poor?

What is helpful to the preacher in remaining humble is what the holy Russian monk Seraphim of Sarov said: "Preaching is easy, it's like throwing stones from the top of a bell tower. What's difficult is putting into practice what one preaches. It's as hard as carrying those same stones on your shoulders, from the ground up to the top of the bell tower."

4. Speaking out of Love

In preaching Christ, the intention can be polluted by other failings as well, including the main one among them, the lack of love. Saint Paul says, "If I speak in human and angelic tongues, but do not have love, I am a resounding gong or a clashing cymbal" (1 Cor 13:1). Experience has made me discover that one can announce Jesus Christ for motives that have little or nothing to do with love. One could do so to proselytize or to find legitimacy for one's own small church or sect, especially if recently founded, by increasing the number of its faithful or could preach to fill the number of chosen ones, to bring the Gospel to the ends of the earth and so hasten the return of the Lord.

Some of these motives are, of course, good and holy; but alone, they are not enough. What is missing is the genuine love and compassion for human beings that is the soul of the Gospel. Why does God send the first missionary, his son Jesus to the world? For no other reason but love: "For God so loved the world that he gave his only Son" (John 3:16). Why did Jesus preach the kingdom? Only for love, for compassion. It was said of Jesus, "[H]is heart was moved with pity for them because they were troubled and abandoned, like sheep without a shepherd" (cf. Matt 9:36; 15:32). The gospel of love can be announced only out of love. If we don't love the people we face, words quickly change in our hands like sharp stones that hurt.

We often resemble Jonah who went to Nineveh to preach, although he didn't like the Ninevites. God had to struggle more to convert him, the preacher, than to convert the inhabitants of Nineveh. Jonah is visibly happier when he can shout, "In forty more days, Nineveh will be destroyed!" than when he must announce the forgiveness of God and the salvation of Nineveh. He's more concerned as well with the castor tree that gives him shade than with the salvation of that city. God says to Jonah, "You are concerned over the plant which cost you no labor and which you did not raise. . . . And should I not be concerned over Nineveh, the great city, in which there are more than a hundred and twenty thousand persons who cannot distinguish their right hand from their left?" (Jonah 4:10-11). From this episode we see that sometimes it's harder for God to convert the preacher than those to whom he sends him to preach.

Love, then, for the people. But even more love for Jesus because the love of Christ must motivate us. The tending and preaching must come out of genuine friendship with Jesus: "[D]o you love me more than these? . . . Feed my lambs" (cf. John 21:15ff.).

Today, especially, love is necessary when ministering to the people. How can we establish the solid validity of the Christian mission and of evangelization within the new context of interreligious dialogue without love? I believe we must go from negative to positive motivation, based on something other than the belief that people will not be saved if they don't get to know Christ.

The apostle Paul helps us discover this when, speaking specifically of the proclamation of the Gospel, he says, "[T]he love of Christ impels us, once we have come to the conviction that one died for all" (2 Cor 5:14). Paul did not announce Christ to avoid peoples' damnation, but because he was moved by the meaning of Christ's vast gift and because he had been "captivated" by him. Not to announce Christ would have seemed to him like hiding a gift, defrauding the world of its due and suffocating the truth. This is what made him exclaim, "Woe to me if I don't preach!"

It is not so much Jesus who is brought to the people, but he who brings himself to the people. The imperative, "The love of Christ impels us," doesn't mean only our love for Christ, but most of all, the love of Christ for us; better, the love of Christ *for all human beings*.

The evangelizing impetus of the Church depends on the place that Jesus Christ occupies in the hearts of Christians. Kierkegaard wrote:

> As God has created man and woman, so too He fashioned the hero and the poet or orator. The poet cannot do what that other does, he can only admire, love and rejoice in the hero. Yet he too is happy, and not less so, for the hero is as it were his better nature, with which he is in love, rejoic-

ing in the fact that this after all is not himself, that his love can be admiration. He is the genius of recollection, can do nothing except call to mind what has been done. . . . He follows the option of his heart, but when he has found what he sought, he wanders before every man's door with his song and with his oration, that all may admire the hero as he does, be proud of the hero as he is.[1]

For this philosopher, the hero is Abraham and the poet is himself, a concept all the more deeply true if we apply it to the hero that is Christ and to the poets and orators that are his announcers. He is the only true hero of history and of the world, because he is also God.

Chapter V

"Of Every Careless Word . . ."

Speaking "as if with Words of God"

1. "Careless" Words and "Effective" Words

In the Gospel of Matthew, in the context of a talk on the words that reveal the heart, there is a saying of Jesus that has made gospel readers of all times tremble: "I tell you, on the day of judgment people will render an account for every careless word they speak" (Matt 12:36).

It has always been difficult to explain what Jesus meant by "careless word." There is some clarification in another passage of Matthew's gospel (7:15-20). Here the same theme of the tree that is recognized by its fruits seems to be directed at the false prophets: "Beware of false prophets, who come to you in sheep's clothing, but underneath are ravenous wolves. By their fruits you will know them."

If the saying of Jesus has some relationship to false prophets, then we can perhaps discover the meaning of the word "careless." The original term translated as "careless" is *argon*, meaning "without effect" (the "a" of deprivation plus *ergon*, "work"). Certain modern translations, while attempting to give a more reassuring meaning to Jesus' threat, explain the term as "unfounded," therefore in the sense of a calumny, but the saying has nothing especially troubling if Jesus says that one has to give account to God of every slander. The meaning of *argon* is rather active, connoting not a word that is *unfounded*, but a word that is *unfounding*, that produces nothing, is empty and powerless.[1] In this sense, the old translation of the Vulgate, *verbum otiosum*, idle word, careless, was more valid and this is the one adopted today in most translations.

It's not difficult to intuit what Jesus means, if we compare this adjective with the one that, in the Bible, constantly typifies the word of God: the adjective *energes*, effective. The word of God is always followed by an effect (*ergon*). Saint Paul, for instance, writes to the Thessalonians that after they received the divine word through the preaching, they accepted it not as a word of men, but as "the word of God, which is now at work [*energeitai*] in you who believe" (cf. 1 Thess 2:13). The opposition between the word of God and human word is presented here, implicitly, like the opposition between the word that is at work and the one that isn't, between the effective word and the word that is ineffective and vain.

Even in the Epistle to the Hebrews we find this notion of the efficacy of the divine word: "the word of God is living and effective [*energes*]" (Heb 4:12). But it's an established concept; in Isaiah, God declares that the word coming out of his mouth never comes back to him "void," without having "achieved the end for which I sent it" (cf. Isa 55:11).

So the useless word, for which people will be accountable on judgment day, is not just every and any careless word; it is the careless, empty word uttered by the person who should instead pronounce the "energetic" words of God. It is therefore the word of the false prophet, who doesn't receive the word of God but nevertheless convinces others to believe that it is the word of God. Human beings, according to the serious admonition of Jesus, will have to be accountable for every careless word about God!

The careless word is the falsification of the word of God, the corruption of that word. It is recognizable by the fruit it doesn't produce, because, by definition, it is sterile, without efficacy. It can please the ear and the intellect, but does not touch the heart, does not move to action. God says he is "watching to fulfill his word" (cf. Jer 1:12); he is jealous of it and cannot allow humankind to take possession of the divine power it holds.

The prophet Jeremiah allows us to hear, as if amplified, the admonishment hidden in the word of Jesus and is clear by now that it concerns the false prophets: "Thus says the LORD of hosts: / Listen not to the words of your prophets, / who fill you with emptiness; / Visions of their own fancy they speak, / not from the mouth of the LORD. . . . / Let the prophet who has a dream recount his dream; let him who has my word speak my word truthfully! / What has straw to do with the wheat? / says the LORD. / Is not my word like fire, says the LORD, / like a hammer shattering rocks? / Therefore I am against the prophets, says the LORD, who steal my words from each other. Yes, I am against the prophets'" (Jer 23:16, 28-31).

2. The False Prophets

But we're not principally here to pursue an investigation of the false prophets of the Bible. The Bible speaks about us and to us, and the word of Jesus does not judge the world, but the Church. The world will not be judged on careless words (all its words, in the sense described above, are careless words) but, rather, for not having believed in Jesus (cf. John 16:9). The men who will be held accountable for every careless word are the men of the Church, we preachers of the word of God.

The false prophets are not only those people who from time to time disseminate heresies; they are also those who are "falsifying the word of God." It is Paul who uses this expression, taking it from current usage; literally, it means to dilute the

Word, as fraudulent innkeepers do when they dilute their wine with water (cf. 2 Cor 2:17; 4:2). False prophets are those who do not present the word of God in all its purity but dilute it with thousands of human words coming from their mouths.

I, too, am a false prophet, every time I don't trust the "weakness" or "pointlessness," the poverty and nudity of the Word, and want to refashion it; anytime I value my embellishment more than the message itself, and I spend more time around that exterior layer than on the Word itself, facing it in prayer, adoring it, and having it live in me. In an absolute sense, of the "real" prophets, there is in fact only one real prophet and he is Jesus Christ, who always and only pronounces "the words of God" (John 3:34). The gospels do not contain even one "careless" word, but only "words of eternal life," words that are "spirit and life."

At Cana of Galilee, Jesus transformed the water into wine, namely, the dead letter into the Spirit that gives life (so the fathers interpret the fact spiritually). The false prophets do the complete opposite, transforming the pure wine of the word of God into water that doesn't inebriate anyone, either in dead letter or in words of human wisdom (cf. 1 Cor 2:4). Deep down, they are ashamed of the Gospel (cf. Rom 1:16) and of the words of Jesus because they are too "hard" for the world and too poor and naked for the scholars, so they try to "flavor" them with what Jeremiah called "the fantasies of their hearts."

Saint Paul wrote to his disciple Timothy, "Be eager to present yourself as acceptable to God, a workman who causes no disgrace, imparting the word of truth without deviation. Avoid profane, idle talk, for such people will become more and more godless" (2 Tim 2:15-16).

Idle and profane chatter does not have any connection to God's design and has nothing to do with the mission of the Church. There are too many human words, too many useless words, too many talks, too many documents going out of the Church! In the era of mass communication, the Church also risks falling into the sea of careless words, said just to be said, written just because there are magazines and newspapers to fill.

In this way, we offer the world an excellent pretext to remain in its disbelief and sin. If an unbeliever were to hear the authentic word of God, it wouldn't be so easy for him to avoid it, saying (as he often does, after hearing our sermons), "Words, words, words!" Saint Paul calls the words of God "the weapons of our battle" and claims that only they "are enormously powerful, capable of destroying fortresses." He continues, "We destroy arguments and every pretension raising itself against the knowledge of God, and take every thought captive in obedience to Christ" (2 Cor 10:3-5).

Humanity is sick from noise, said the philosopher Kierkegaard. We must call for a fast, but a fast in words; someone has to cry out, as Moses did one day, "Be silent, O Israel, and listen!" (Deut 27:9). Pope Benedict XVI remembered the need for this "fast of words" in one of his Lenten meetings with the parish priests of Rome, and I think that, as always, his invitation was directed at the Church even before the world.

3. "Jesus Did not Come to Tell Us Fairy Tales"

It's worthwhile meditating on these words by Péguy:

> Jesus Christ, my child,
> —it's the Church that addresses her children—,
> didn't come to tell us fairy tales . . .
> He didn't make the journey down to earth
> to tell us riddles and jokes.
> He did not have the time to joke around . . .
> He did not spend his life . . .
> To come and tell us nonsense stories.[2]

The concern for keeping the word of God distinct from every other word is such that, in sending his apostles out on a mission, Jesus orders them not to greet anyone along the way (cf. Luke 10:4). I have experienced, at my own expense, that at times this command must be taken literally. Stopping to greet people and exchange pleasantries while one is about to preach inevitably disperses concentration on the word to announce and makes one lose a sense of his distinctiveness in relationship to any human talk. It's the same need we experience (or should experience) when getting dressed to celebrate Mass.

The need is even stronger when it's not a matter of the preliminaries, but of the very content of preaching. In the Gospel of Mark, Jesus quotes the words of Isaiah: "This people draws near with words only / and honors me with their lips alone, . . . / And their reverence for me has become / routine observance of the precepts of men" (Isa 29:13); then he adds, turning toward the Pharisees and scribes, "You disregard God's commandment but cling to human tradition. . . . How well you have set aside the commandment of God in order to uphold your tradition!" (Mark 7:7-13).

When we're not able to propose the simple and naked word of God, without the filter of a thousand distinctions and clarifications, additions and explanations, right as they may be but diminishing the power of God, we do the very thing that Jesus reproached to the Pharisees and the scribes, we "nullify the word of God" and "ensnare" it, making it lose a large part of its power to penetrate the hearts of people.

The word of God cannot be used for special occasion speeches or to embellish with divine authority and a few biblical quotes talks already shaped and totally based in human content. In recent times, we have seen where this tendency leads us, and the gospel has been made an instrument to sustain all kinds of human endeavors.

When an audience is so predetermined by psychological, political, or emotional conditioning to make it impossible from the start not to say what it expects to hear, when there is no hope of being able to bring the listeners to a point when you can say to them, "Convert and believe!"—then it's good not to proclaim the word of God at all so that it not be used for biased motives and so be betrayed. In other words, it's better to give up making a real, concrete announcement. It may be better to simply listen, trying to understand and take part in people's anxieties and suffering, preaching rather the Gospel of the kingdom with one's presence and with charity. In the gospel, Jesus is very careful not to become an instrument for political or partisan ends.

In dealing with the doctrinal and disciplinary problems of the Church, one must have the courage to start from the word of God, especially that of the New Testament, and to remain more closely tied to it; in this way one will be much more certain to reach the purpose of discovering, in each question, the will of God.

The same need is felt in religious communities. At times, in educating young people and novices, in spiritual exercises, and in other aspects of communal life, it happens that more time is spent on the writings of one's own founder or foundress (often, frankly, quite trite and poor in content) than on the word of God. And disciples of men and women are formed before disciples of Christ.

4. Speaking as if with Words of God

I realize that what I'm saying can give rise to a serious objection. So, the preaching of the Church will have to be reduced to a sequence (or deluge) of biblical quotes, with so many picky indications of book, chapter, and verse, just like the Jehovah's Witnesses and other fundamentalist groups? Certainly not. We are heirs to a different tradition. I'll explain what I mean by remaining bound to the word of God.

In the Second Letter to the Corinthians, Saint Paul writes, "For we are not like the many who trade on the word of God; but as out of sincerity, indeed as from God and in the presence of God, we speak in Christ" (2 Cor 2:17), and Saint Peter, in his first letter, exhorts Christians, saying, "Whoever preaches, let it be with the words of God" (1 Pet 4:11). What does "speaking in Christ" mean, or to speak "as if with words of God"? It surely does not mean to repeat, materially and only, words said by Christ and God in Scripture. It means that the basic inspiration, the thought that "informs" and supports all the rest, must come from God, not from man. The preacher must be "moved by God" and speak as if in his presence.

There are two ways to prepare a sermon or any other announcement of faith, oral or written. First, I can sit down at a desk and choose by myself the words to say, the theme to develop, based on my knowledge and my preferences. Then, once the talk is ready, I can kneel and ask God quickly to bless what I've written and give efficacy to my words. It is something good, but it's not, however, the prophetic way. One has to do the opposite. First, kneel down and ask God what word he wants to say; then, sit at a desk and use one's knowledge to shape that word. This changes everything, because it's not God who has to make my word his, but I who make his word mine.

We must start from the certainty of faith that, in every circumstance, the risen Lord has in his heart a word that he wishes to communicate to his people. The Risen One did not write the seven letters only to seven Churches of Asia Minor. He continues to send "letters" to every Church. That's what changes things and what we must discover, and he does not

60

fail to reveal it to his minister, if he asks humbly and persistently. At first his word is an almost imperceptible movement of the heart, a small light that goes on in the mind, a word of the Bible that begins to attract attention and illuminates a situation. It is truly "the tiniest of all seeds," but later you realize that everything was enclosed in it; there was a thunder big enough to break apart the cedars of Lebanon. Later, you sit at your desk, open your books, consult your notes, consult the fathers of the Church, the teachers, the poets. But by now it's something completely different. It's no longer the Word of God at the service of your culture, but your culture at the service of the Word of God.

Origen describes well the process that leads to this discovery. He said that before finding nourishment in Scripture, one must sustain a certain "poverty of the senses; from every angle the soul is surrounded by darkness and it encounters roads without an exit. But suddenly, after deep research and prayer, the voice of the Word resounds, and immediately something lights up; the one he was seeking goes toward the soul 'jumping over the mountains and leaping on the hills' (cf. Ct 2, 8), namely opening the mind to receive one of his strong and luminous words."[3] This moment brings with it great joy, leading Jeremiah to say, "When I found your words, I devoured them; / they became my joy and the happiness of my heart" (Jer 15:16).

Usually, God's answer comes in the form of a word of Scripture, which in that moment reveals its incredible relevance to the situation and to the problem to be dealt with, as if written especially for it. At times, it's not even necessary to explicitly quote the biblical word or comment on it. It's enough that it be present in the mind of the speaker and that it inform all that is said. In this way, he speaks, in fact, "as if with words of God." This method is always valid: for important documents as well as for lessons given by the teacher to his novices, for a scholarly conference and a modest Sunday homily alike.

Therefore, human reality and experience are not excluded from the preaching of the Church, but they must be submitted to and at the service of the word of God. Just as in the Eucharist, the body of Christ, spiritually speaking, assimilates the person who eats it and not vice-versa, so in preaching, the word of God must be the strongest vital principle that subjugates and assimilates human words, and not the contrary.

The great religious orator, Bossuet, writes: "The evangelical preacher is one who makes Jesus Christ speak. He must not indulge in a human language so as not to give an extraneous body to the eternal truth. He doesn't disdain—as St. Augustine says—the embellishments of human eloquence when they're appropriate, but neither is he concerned with making excessive use of them. Every means seems good only if it's a mirror in which Jesus Christ and his truth are reflected, a channel from which emerge the pure and living waters of the Gospel. Or, if something more spirited is desired, the preacher is a faithful interpreter who does not alter, does not mislead or weaken his holy word, nor is mingled with it."[4]

We have all had the experience of the power of a single word of God deeply believed and felt by the person pronouncing it, and often unbeknownst to him. Often we have to realize that, among so many other words, it has been that particular one that has touched the heart and led more than one listener to repentance.

In my service as Sunday commentator of the Gospel on television, I have gathered many testimonials, such as the one of an engaged couple whose philosophy was to enjoy life to the maximum without any limits or rules. Their parents invited them to a mission day and they accepted politely without taking the event at all seriously. During the sermon, they heard these words being said: "Wide is the road that leads to perdition." The young woman was thunderstruck and turned to her fiancé, saying, "We are walking down that wide road. . . . Either you also change, or we will no longer be seeing each other." Furious, he answered that she had lost her mind, he would take her home, and then say goodbye! But something happened to him as well. One day he opened the Bible and read, "I stand at the door knocking," and again, the word of God performed a miracle. Today, married and with a number of children, they are lay missionaries involved in spreading the Gospel in a diocese of Southern Italy.

After having pointed to the conditions of the Christian announcement (to speak of Christ with sincerity, as if moved by God under his glance), the Apostle wondered, "Who is qualified for this?" (2 Cor 2:16). Clearly, no one is up to this. We hold this treasure in earthen vessels (2 Cor 4:7). We can, however, pray and say, "Lord, have mercy on this poor earthen pot that must carry the treasure of your word; keep us from pronouncing careless words when speaking of you; let us once experience the taste of your word so that we can distinguish it from all other words and so that all other words seem tasteless to us. As you promised, spread hunger throughout the land, "Not a famine of bread, or thirst for water, / but for hearing the word of the LORD'" (Amos 8:11).

Chapter VI

"Welcome the Word"

The Word of God, Path to Personal Sanctification

1. Lectio Divina

In this chapter, we reflect on the word of God as a path to personal sanctification. The *Lineamenta*, compiled in preparation for the work of the bishops' synod (October 2008), treats this topic in chapter 2, especially in the part devoted to "the word of God in the life of the believer."

It's a theme dear to the spiritual tradition of the Church. Saint Ambrose said, "The word of God is the vital substance of our soul, it nourishes and governs it; there is no other thing that can make the soul of man live, except the word of God."[1] And *Dei Verbum* adds: "And such is the force and power of the Word of God that it can serve the Church as her support and vigor, and the children of the Church as strength for their faith, food for the soul, and a pure and lasting fount of spiritual life."[2]

John Paul II wrote in the *Novo millennio ineunte*, "It is necessary that the hearing of the Word becomes a vital encounter, in the ancient and always valid *lectio divina* that allows us to pick out of the biblical text the living word that questions, orients and molds existence."[3] Pope Benedict XVI also expressed himself on this theme, on the occasion of the International Congress of Sacred Scripture in the life of the Church: "The regular reading of holy Scripture, accompanied by prayer, realizes that intimate dialogue where in reading, we listen to God who speaks and in praying, we answer him with a trustful opening of the heart."[4]

With the following reflections, I place myself in this rich tradition, starting from what Scripture itself tells us about this issue. In the letter to Saint James, we read this famous text on the word of God:

> He willed to give us birth by the word of truth that we may be a kind of first fruits of his creatures. Know this, my dear brothers: everyone should be quick to hear, slow to speak, slow to wrath. . . . Therefore, put away all filth and evil excess and humbly welcome the word that has been planted in you and is able to save your souls. Be doers of the word and not hearers only, deluding yourselves. For if anyone is a hearer of the word and not a doer, he is like a man who looks at his own face in a mirror. He sees himself, then goes off and promptly forgets what he looked like. But the one who peers into the perfect law of freedom and perseveres, and is not a hearer who forgets but a doer who acts, such a one shall be blessed in what he does. (Jas 1:18-25)

Some themes return almost word for word in the other famous text on the word of God by 1 Peter 1:23–2:2. James says that "He [God] willed to give us birth by the word of truth" (Jas 1:18); and in 1 Peter it is said that Christians "have been reborn anew, not from perishable but from imperishable seed, through the living and abiding word of God." Both start from the fundamental and mysterious fact of baptism and base every further moral discussion on it.

Saint James encourages us to cast off every moral impurity, to welcome with docility the word already sown in us; and Saint Peter, almost with the same words, says: "Rid yourselves of all malice and all deceit, insincerity, envy, and all slander; like newborn infants, long for pure spiritual milk" (1 Pet 2:1-2). The two apostles tell us that in coming close to the word of God, we must feel the same need to be purified from sin that we experience in receiving the body of Christ.

2. Welcoming the Word

From the text of James, we derive a plan of *lectio divina* made of three consecutive stages or parts: receiving the word, meditating on the word, putting the word into practice.

So the first step is the hearing of the word: "Accept with docility the seed that has been planted in you." The image of the seed recalls the parable of the sower ("The seed is the word of God"; Luke 8:11) and is a tacit invitation to be among those who embrace the word "with a generous and good heart, and bear fruit through perseverance" (Luke 8:15).

This first stage embraces all the forms and ways in which a Christian comes into contact with the word of God, first by listening to the word in the liturgy, which is now made easier by the use of the vernacular and the wise choice of texts distributed throughout the year. Then there are biblical schools, written aids, and, the personal, irreplaceable reading of the Bible at home. In *Dei Verbum* we read, "The sacred Synod forcefully and specifically exhorts all the faithful, especially those who live the religious life, to learn 'the surpassing knowledge of Jesus Christ' (Phil 3:8) by frequent reading of divine Scriptures. . . . Therefore let them go gladly to the sacred text itself, whether in the sacred liturgy, which is full of the divine words, or in devout reading, or in such suitable exercises and various other helps."[5] For those who make Scripture the field of their personal scientific research, they can add to it the systematic study of the Bible, exegesis, textual criticism, biblical theology, and the study of the original languages.

In this stage, it's important to be aware of two dangers. The first is to stop at this first phase and transform one's personal reading of the word of God into an "impersonal" reading. This danger is very strong today, especially in places of academic formation. Kierkegaard observes that if individuals expect to be personally questioned by the Word, until they have resolved all the problems connected to the text, the variants and the divergences of opinion of scholars, nothing will be accomplished. In fact, this becomes a ruse to stay guarded against the word of God. This was given to us so that we put it into practice and not work at the exegesis of its difficulties. There is an "inflation of hermeneutics," and, worse yet, we believe that the most serious thing about the Bible is its hermeneutics, not its practice.

"Oh, what a depth of shrewdness! The word of God reduced to something impersonal, objective, to a doctrine, instead of being the voice of God that you must listen to."[6] It's not the obscure points of the Bible that scare me, it's the clear ones, the same philosopher said.

Saint James compares the reading of the word of God to looking at oneself in the mirror. But, Kierkegaard observes, those who limit themselves to study the sources, the variants, the literary genres of the Bible, and nothing else, are like those who spend all their time contemplating the mirror, examining its form, material, style, without ever *looking at oneself* in the mirror. For those individuals, the mirror does not perform its proper function.

The critical study of the word of God is indispensable; we are never sufficiently grateful to those who spend their lives clearing the way to an always better understanding of the sacred text. Yet this alone does not exhaust the meaning of Scripture; it's necessary, but not sufficient.

The other danger is fundamentalism: taking literally all that is read in the Bible, without any mediation of interpretation. This second risk is much less harmless than might at first appear, as is dramatically seen in the current debate on creationism, intelligent design, and theistic evolution.

Those who defend the literal reading of Genesis (the world created, just as it is today, in six days, some thousands of years ago) cause deep damage to the faith. The scientific researcher and believer, Francis Collins, director of the project that created the mapping of the human genome, wrote, "Young people brought up in homes and Churches that insist on creationism, sooner or later encounter the overwhelming scientific evidence in favor of an ancient universe and the relatedness of all living things through the process of evolution and natural selection. What a terrible and unnecessary dilemma they then face! To adhere to the faith of their childhood, they are required to reject a broad and rigorous body of scientific data, effectively committing intellectual suicide. Presented with no other alternative than Creationism, is it any wonder that many of these young people turn away from faith, concluding that they simply cannot believe in a God who would ask them to reject what science has so compellingly taught us about the natural world?"[7]

This problem is especially acute in the United States, where many groups inspired by fundamentalism operate, but it's present even elsewhere in other forms. These two extremes, of hyper-criticism and fundamentalism, are opposites only in appearance. They have in common the act of stopping at the letter, neglecting the Spirit.

Psalm 39 : 23-24

3. Contemplating the Word

The second stage suggested by Saint James consists in "fixating the eyes," or meditating on the word, by staying at length in front of the mirror. In this regard, the fathers evoke images of chewing and ruminating as illustrated by Guigo II, the theoretician of _lectio divina_: "Reading, as it were, puts food whole in the mouth, meditation chews it and breaks it up."[8] Saint Augustine adds, "When one recalls the things heard and sweetly thinks of them in his heart, he becomes similar to the ruminant."[9]

The soul that sees itself in the mirror of the Word learns to know "how it is," learns to know itself, and discovers its deformity from the image of God and the image of Christ. "I do not seek my own glory," Jesus says (John 8:50): well, the mirror is in front of you and immediately you see how far you are from Jesus. "Blessed are the poor in spirit" (Matt 5:3): the mirror is again in front of you and immediately you see that you are full of attachments and full of superfluous things. "Charity is patient" (1 Cor 13:4) and you realize how impatient, envious, and self-interested you are.

More than to "search the Scriptures" (cf. John 5:39), you must let yourself *be searched* by Scripture. The letter to the Hebrews says, "Indeed, the word of God is living and effective, sharper than any two-edged sword, penetrating even between soul and spirit, joints and marrow, and able to discern reflections and thoughts of the heart. No creature is concealed from him, but everything is naked and exposed to the eyes of him to whom we must render an account" (Heb 4:12-13). The best prayer with which to start the moment of contemplation of the Word is to repeat with the Psalmist:

> Probe me, God, know my heart;
>   try me, know my concerns.
> See if my way is crooked,
>   then lead me in the ancient paths. (Ps 139:23-24)

In the mirror of the Word, we see the face of God as well as ourselves, and see beyond to *the heart* of God. Gregory the Great says, "Scripture is a letter of almighty God to his creature; in it, one learns to know the heart of God in the words of God."[10] The saying of Jesus is valid even for God, "[F]rom the fullness of the heart the mouth speaks" (Matt 12:34). In

69

Scripture, God speaks to us about what fills his heart, which is love. All the Scriptures are written so that humankind could understand how much God loves all and could understand it in order to burn with love for him.[11]

Contemplation of the Word provides us with the two most important forms of knowledge to advance on the road to true wisdom: the knowledge of self and the knowledge of God. Saint Augustine said to God, "May I know myself and may I know you; that I may know myself as to become humble and that I may know you so as to love you."[12] And Saint Francis was used to spending nights repeating, "Who are you, Lord, and who am I?" Both are equally necessary. Knowledge of God without knowledge of self leads to presumption; knowledge of self without knowledge of God can lead to dispair.

A very beautiful example of this double knowledge of self and God that is obtained from the word of God is the letter to the Church of Laodicea in the book of Revelation. The Risen One, first of all, lays bare the real situation of the typical faithful of this community, saying, "I know your works; I know that you are neither cold nor hot. . . . So, because you are lukewarm, neither hot nor cold, I will spit you out of my mouth." An impressive contrast between what the people think of themselves and what God thinks of them: "For you say, 'I am rich and affluent and have no need of anything,' and yet do not realize that you are wretched, pitiable, poor, blind, and naked" (Rev 3:14-20).

Such an unusual harshness is soon overturned by one of the most touching descriptions of the love of God: "Behold, I stand at the door and knock. If anyone hears my voice and opens the door, [then] I will enter his house and dine with him, and he with me." This is an image that reveals its realistic, not only metaphoric, meaning if it's read thinking about the eucharistic banquet (as the liturgical context of Revelation suggests). Knowledge of one's own poverty and knowledge of the invincible love of God!

This page of Revelation can help us verify the personal state of our soul and also lay bare the spiritual condition of a large part of modern society. It is similar to one of those infrared photos taken from an artificial satellite, revealing a landscape completely different from the habitual one, under natural light. Even this world of ours, strong in its scientific and technical conquests (as the Laodicians were in their commercial fortunes), feels satisfied, rich, not needing anyone, not even God. Yet someone must let the world know the true diagnosis of its state: "You do not know that you are wretched, pitiable, poor, blind, and naked. " Someone has to cry out, just like the child in the Anderson fairy tale, "The king is naked!" But done out of love and with love, as the Risen One does with the Laodicians.

For this discovery of ourselves and of God in the Word, we have a precious aid within us, an interpreter always available, not on the outside, but inside of us: our soul. There is a certain affinity between our soul and Scripture: both carry within the image of God, therefore one can help to understand the other. The mirror that is our soul, though, contrary to the mirror of Scripture, is no longer pure, it's darkened by sin, like a well filled with ground and debris. This is why Saint James and Saint Peter urged us to "put down every impurity and malice" as we approach the word of God. This is why a constant purification of the heart is necessary in order to receive the Word.

Commenting on the word of Proverbs that says, "Drink water from your own cistern, / running water from your own well" (Prov 5:15), Origen wrote, "You too must attempt to have your own well and your own spring, so that when you take up a book of the Scriptures, you may begin even from your understanding, to bring forth some meaning, and in accordance with those things which you have learned in church, you too must attempt to drink from the fountain of your own abilities. You have a kind of 'living water' within you. Within

71

you there are perennial veins and streams flowing with rational understanding, as long as they have not been filled up with earth and rubbish. But get busy to dig your earth and to clean out the filth, that is, to remove the idleness of your natural ability and cast out the inactivity of your heart."[13]

Experience shows that often a simple soul in prayer grasps the truth and interconnections of the word of God that had escaped very skilled commentators full of technical knowledge about Scripture. We should therefore not be resigned to depend only and exclusively on the explanations of others or that we read somewhere. We must also seek "within us" with humility and confidence.

The word of God assures each soul that wants it, a fundamental and intrinsically infallible spiritual direction. There is always, so to speak, an extraordinary spiritual direction that comes forth in special moments, when faced with making radical decisions and choices. Often even in such cases, God has revealed his will through a word of the Bible heard by chance or sought purposely. Even today, many Christians experience these "decisive" words of God that have in themselves the strength to produce turning points to one's life.

But there is also an ordinary and daily spiritual direction that consists in discovering what God wants in various life situations, both human and spiritual, in which people usually find themselves. This direction is assured by meditation on the word of God, accompanied by an interior unction of the Spirit that translates the word into good "inspiration" and good inspiration into a practical resolution. This is expressed by that verse of the psalm very dear to the lovers of the Word: "Your word is a lamp for my feet, / a light for my path" (Ps 119:105).

I was once preaching during a mission in Australia. On the last day a man came to see me, an Italian migrant working there, and he told me, "Father, I have a serious problem: my eleven-year-old son has not been baptized. My wife became a Jehovah's Witness and wants nothing to do with baptism in the Catholic Church. If I baptize him, there will be a crisis and if I don't, I won't feel at peace. When we married, we were both Catholics and promised to educate our children in the faith. What should I do?" I said, "Let me think about it over tonight, come back tomorrow and we'll see what we can do." The next day, the man returned visibly more peaceful and told me, "Father, I found the solution. Last night, upon returning home, I prayed for a while and then opened the Bible. I came to the passage where Abraham takes his son to be immolated and I saw that when he did so, he didn't say anything to his wife." It was a perfect discernment on his part. I baptized the boy myself and it was a moment of great joy for all.

This act of opening the Bible is a delicate thing, it must be done with discretion, in a climate of faith and after having prayed at length. It's undeniable that under these conditions the process has often given marvelous fruits and has been practiced even by the saints. In the sources, we read that Saint Francis of Assisi discovered the kind of life God was calling him to, opening the gospel by chance "after having devoutly prayed" with his companions who were "willing to accept the first advice that would be offered them."[14] Augustine interprets the words he heard from a neighboring house, *"Tolle lege"* (take and read), as a divine order to open the book of the letters of Paul and to read the first verse that would appear to his eyes.[15]

There have been souls that became saintly simply with the spiritual direction of the word of God. Saint Therese of Lisieux wrote, "In the gospel I find everything needful for my poor soul. In it I constantly discover new lights, hidden and mysterious meanings. I understand and know from experience that: 'the kingdom of God is within us' (cf. Luke 17:21). Jesus does not need books or doctors to teach souls; he is the Doctor of doctors, he teaches without the sound of words."[16] It was through the word of God, reading one chapter after the other,

12 and 13 of the First Letter to the Corinthians, that the saint discovered her deep vocation and exclaimed, jubilantly, "In the mystical body of Christ I will be the heart that loves!"

The Bible offers us a vivid image of everything that has been said to us about meditating on the word: the image of the devoured book that we read in Ezekiel:

> It was then I saw a hand stretched out to me, in which was a written scroll which he unrolled before me. It was covered with writing front and back, and written on it was: Lamentation and wailing and woe!
>
> He said to me: Son of man, eat what is before you; eat this scroll, then go, speak to the house of Israel. So I opened my mouth and he gave me the scroll to eat. Son of man, he then said to me, feed your belly and fill your stomach with this scroll I am giving you. I ate it, and it was as sweet as honey in my mouth. (Ezek 2:9–3:3)

The theme is inaugurated by Jeremiah ("When I found your words, I devoured them"; Jer 15:16) and is picked up again by the author of Revelation (Rev 10:8-10). There is an enormous difference between the book simply read or studied and the book devoured. In the second case, the Word truly becomes—as Saint Ambrose used to say—"the substance of our soul," that which informs our thoughts, forms our language, determines our actions, creates "the spiritual" man. The word that is ingested is a word "assimilated" by mankind. However, it is a passive assimilation like in the case of the Eucharist, namely, "a being assimilated" by the Word, subjugated and conquered by it, which is the strongest vital principle.

In the contemplation of the word, we have a most sweet model, that of "Mary [who] kept all these things [literally: these words], reflecting on them in her heart" (Luke 2:19). In her the metaphor of the devoured book has also become a physical reality. The Word has literally "filled her womb."

4. Doing the Word

And so we arrive at the third stage of the path suggested by the apostle James, the one on which he most insists: "Be among those who put the word into practice . . . if one only listens and doesn't put into practice; . . . he who puts it into practice, will find his happiness in practicing it." It is also what is closest to Jesus' heart: "My mother and my brothers are those who hear the word of God and act on it" (Luke 8:21). Without this "doing the Word," everything remains an illusion, a building made on sand. Nor can one be said to have understood the Word because, as Gregory the Great writes, the word of God is truly understood only when one begins to practice it.[17]

This third phase consists, practically, in obeying the Word. The Greek term used in the New Testament to designate obedience (*hypakouein*) translated literally means to "listen to," in the sense of accomplishing what one has heard. "But my people did not *listen to* my words; / Israel did not *obey* me," God laments in the Bible (Ps 81:12; emphasis added). In its most original meaning, therefore, obeying means being submitted to the word, recognizing its real power on you, not only theoretically, but practically, namely, doing what the Word commands or suggests.

As soon as we try to find, throughout the New Testament, in what consists the duty of obedience, we make a surprising discovery, that obedience is almost always seen as obedience to God's word. Saint Paul speaks of obedience to the *teaching* (Rom 6:17), of obedience to the *gospel* (Rom 10:16; 2 Thess 1:8), of obedience to *the truth* (Gal 5:7), of obedience to *Christ* (2 Cor 10:5). We find the same language elsewhere as well: the Acts of the Apostles speak of obedience to *faith* (Acts 6:7), and the First Letter of Peter speaks of obedience to *Christ* (1 Pet 1:2) and obedience to *truth* (1 Pet 1:22).

The obedience of Jesus himself works especially through obedience to written words. In the passage of the temptation in the desert, Jesus' obedience lies in recalling the words of God and keeping to them: "It is written"! His obedience works particularly on the words that are written about him and for him "in the law, in the prophets and in the psalms." As man, he discovers them gradually as he advances in the understanding and the accomplishment of his mission. Jesus says to those who are opposed to his capture: "But then how would the scriptures be fulfilled which say that it must come to pass in this way?" (Matt 26:54). The life of Jesus is guided by a luminous trail not seen by others and formed by the words written for him; he infers from the Scriptures the "what must be" (*dei*) that governs his whole life.

The words of God, under the actual action of the Holy Spirit, become an expression of the living will of God for me, in a given moment. A small example will help us to understand better than a lot of explanations. On one occasion, I realized that an object I normally used had disappeared. I was just about to make this known and ask for its return when, by chance (but maybe not really by chance), I fell upon the word of Jesus that says, "Give to everyone who asks of you, and from the one who takes what is yours do not demand it back" (Luke 6:30). I understood that this word did not apply universally and to all cases, but certainly it applied to me in that moment. I have to confess that I didn't come out smelling like a rose.

Obedience to the word of God is the obedience we can have at all times. Once in a while, three or four times in a lifetime, we might, for serious cases, be obedient to visible orders and authority. But for obedience to the word of God, it can happen every minute. It's also the obedience that we can *all* have, underlings and superiors, clerics and laypersons. The latter don't have, in the Church, a superior to obey (in the same sense that religious and clerics have). But they have instead "a Lord" to obey! They have his word!

Hence we understand how, to rediscover the word of God in today's Church, we must follow closely a rediscovery of obedience. We cannot cultivate the word of God, without also cultivating obedience. Otherwise, we become *ipso facto* disobedient. To "disobey" (*parakouein*) means to listen poorly, inattentively. We could also say it means to listen with detachment, in a neutral way, without feeling bound to what one is hearing, preserving our power of decision in front of the Word.

Let us end our meditation with the same prayer that Saint Augustine elevates to God in his *Confessions*, to obtain the understanding of the word of God: "Let your Scriptures be my chaste delight. Let me neither be deceived in them nor deceive others by them. . . . Listen to my soul and hear its cry from its depths. . . . Grant me a space for my meditation on the hidden things of your law, and do not close your law against me when I knock. For it was not for nothing that you willed that so many pages should be filled with the writing of such dark secrets. . . . O Lord, perfect me and reveal those pages to me! See, your voice gives me joy; your voice surpasses all abundance of pleasures. Give me what I love . . . do not forsake your grass that is thirsty for you. . . . May the inner secrets of your words be laid open to me when I knock. This I beg by our Lord Jesus Christ . . . in whom are hidden all the treasures and knowledge (Col 2:3). These are the treasures I seek in your books."[18]

Chapter VII

"The Letter Brings Death, the Spirit Gives Life"

The Spiritual Reading of the Bible

1. Scripture Divinely Inspired

In the Second Letter to Timothy is found the famous affirmation, "All Scripture is inspired by God" (2 Tim 3:16). In the original language, the expression translated with "inspired by God" or "divinely inspired" is one word only, *theopneustos*, which contains the two words: God (*Theos*) and Spirit (*Pneuma*). This word has two basic meanings: one very well known and the other usually neglected, although not less important than the first.

The most well-known meaning is the passive one, brought to light in all the modern translations: Scripture is "inspired by God." Another passage in the New Testament explains the meaning in this way: "human beings [the prophets] moved by the holy Spirit spoke under the influence of God" (2 Pet 1:21). It is actually the classical doctrine of divine inspiration of the Scriptures, the one we proclaim as an article of faith in the Credo, when we say that the Holy Spirit is the one that "has spoken through the prophets."

This doctrine brings us to the very source of the whole Christian mystery, the Trinity, namely, the oneness and the distinction of the three Divine Persons. The Holy Spirit accompanies the Word, as, within the Trinity, the breath of the Holy Spirit is tied to the generation of the Word. Just like in the incarnation the Spirit comes to Mary so that the Word be made flesh in her womb, in the same (but not identical) way the Spirit functions in the holy writer so that he receives the word of God and embodies it in a human language.

We can represent for ourselves with human images this mysterious inspiration: God, with his divine finger—that is, with his living energy that is the Holy Spirit—"touches" that remote point where the human spirit opens up to the infinite; from there, that very simple and immediate touch that God produces, spreads like a resonant vibration to all the human faculties—will, intelligence, imagination, heart, transforming itself into concepts, images, words. Then occurs the mysterious passage from divine movement to created reality that is observed in all the works *ad extra* of God: in creation, in the incarnation, in the production of grace.

In this manner, we obtain a theandric reality, namely, fully divine and fully human; the two elements intimately fused, even if not "confused." In the encyclicals *Providentissimus Deus* by Leo XIII and *Divino Afflante Spiritu* of Pius XII, the magisterium of the Church tells us that the two elements, divine and human, have been kept intact. God is the main author because he assumes responsibility for what is written and determines its content with the action of its Spirit. Yet the sacred writer is also the author in the full sense of the word, because he has closely collaborated in this action through a normal human activity that God used like an instrument. The fathers said that God is like the musician who, touching the cords of the lyre, makes them vibrate; the sound is completely produced by the musician but it would not exist without the cords of the lyre.

Usually, only one effect of this marvelous work of God is brought to light: the biblical lack of error, namely, the fact that the Bible does not contain any error (if by error we correctly mean the absence of a humanly possible truth, in a certain cultural context and therefore accountable by the person

79

writing). But biblical inspiration establishes much more than simply the lack of error of the word of God (that is something negative); it establishes in a positive way, its inexhaustibility, its strength and divine vitality and what Augustine called the *mira profunditas*, its marvelous depth.[1]

Now we're prepared to discover that other less well-known meaning of biblical inspiration, that I was describing earlier. Grammatically, in itself, the participle *theopneustos* is active, not passive, and if it's true that tradition and theology have always explained it in a passive sense (inspired by God), it is also true that the same tradition has also been able to capture in it an active sense. Saint Ambrose said that Scripture is *theopneustos* not only in the sense that it is "inspired by God" but also in the sense that it "inspires God," it breathes God![2]

Speaking of creation, Augustine said that God did not make things and then leave but that "coming from him, they remain in Him."[3] So it is of the words of God: having come from him, they remain in him and he in them. After dictating Scripture, the Holy Spirit enclosed itself in it, lives in it, and animates it constantly with its divine breath. Heidegger said that "the word is the home of Being"; we can say that the Word (with a capital letter) is the home of the Spirit.

The conciliar constitution *Dei Verbum* also embodies this vein of tradition when it claims that because the holy Scriptures "are inspired by God [passive inspiration!] and committed to writing once and for all time, they present God's own word in an unalterable form, and they make the voice of the Holy Spirit sound again and again in the words of the prophets and apostles [active inspiration!]."[4]

Once again, we must realize the marvelous relationship between the mystery of the Eucharist and that of the word of God. In the Mass, through the epiclesis and the consecration, the Holy Spirit first gives us the Eucharist and later, in communion, the Eucharist gives us the Holy Spirit. In the beginning and once and for all, the Holy Spirit has inspired Scripture and now every time we open it, Scripture breathes the Holy Spirit! These are inspirations that move our will toward the good, illuminations that light up our mind, affections of the heart.

2. Biblical Docetism and Ebionism

But now we must face the most delicate issue of how we can approach the Scriptures so that they can really "free up" for us the Spirit they contain. How can we "explain" Scriptures or—taking this term literally—how can we penetrate within its folds so that they exude that divine fragrance that, through faith, we know is to be found there? I said that Scripture is a theandric reality, namely divine-human. Now the law of every theandric reality (for instance, Christ and the Church) is that you can't discover the divine in it except by passing through the human. We cannot discover the divinity of Christ if not through his concrete humanity.

In antiquity, those who believed differently fell into Docetism. Scorning the body and physical marks of Christ as simple "appearances" (*dokein*), they also lost his deep reality and in place of a living God-made-man, they were left with a fanciful idea of God. In the same way, we cannot discover the Spirit in the Scriptures if not going through the letter, meaning through the concrete sheath that the word of God has taken on in various books and inspired authors. We cannot discover the divine meaning in it if not starting from the human significance, as understood by the human authors Isaiah, Jeremiah, Luke, Paul, etc.

The vast effort of study and research surrounding the book of Scripture finds its full justification in this fact. There are large groups of faithful who spend their life shedding light

81

on the problems of the Bible, issues concerning the very text of the Scriptures, the historical and cultural context of each book, the various literary genres, the internal and external sources of the Bible and the precise meaning of each passage. The Christian people owe a debt of gratitude to these brothers and sisters; in opening our Bible, without even realizing it, we gather the full fruits of their labor and are enriched by it.

But fundamentalism is not the only problem facing biblical exegesis. Jesus was one of my examples: not only was the problem of Docetism, the neglect of the human aspect, facing the person of Jesus. There was also the danger of stopping there, of seeing only the human side to him and not discovering the divine dimension of the Son of God. In other words, there was the danger of Ebionism. For the Ebionists (who were Judeo-Christian), Jesus was, yes, if you will, a great prophet, possibly the greatest, but nothing more. The fathers called them "Ebionites" (from *ebionim*, "the poor") to say that they were poor in faith.

The same thing happens for the Scriptures. There is a biblical Ebionism, the danger of stopping at the letter, considering the Bible an excellent book, the most excellent of human books, if you will, but still a purely human book. Unfortunately, we run the risk of reducing Scripture to one dimension. The rupture of unity, today, does not lean toward Docetism, but toward Ebionism.

Kierkegaard wrote these words that, even after a century and a half, maintain a good part of their validity, even for Catholics: "How is God's word read in Christendom? If we were to distinguish two classes (for we cannot here concern ourselves with individual exceptions), one might say that the greater part never read God's word, and that a smaller part read it learnedly in one fashion or another, that is to say, do not really read God's word, but admire the mirror. Or, to say the same thing in another way, the greater part regard God's word as an antiquated document which one puts aside, and a smaller part regards God's word as an exceedingly notable document of olden time upon which one expends an astonishing amount of diligence and acumen."[5]

Many scholars explain the Bible intentionally with only the historico-critical method. I don't mean the nonbelieving scholars for whom this is normal, but the scholars who profess to be believers. In no case has the secularization of the sacred revealed itself to be so acute as the secularization of the sacred Book. Now, to pretend to understand Scripture exhaustively, studying it only with the instrument of historico-philological analysis, is like pretending to discover what the Eucharist is, based on a chemical analysis of the consecrated host! This type of analysis, even if it were pushed to the maximum of perfection, really only represents the first step in the knowledge of the Bible, the one that pertains to the letter.

Jesus solemnly affirms in the gospel that "Abraham . . . rejoiced to see my day" (John 8:56), that "he [Moses] wrote about me" (John 5:46), that Isaiah "saw his glory and spoke about him" (John 12:41), that the prophets and the psalms and all Scripture speak of him (cf. Luke 24:27, 44; John 5:39). But today, the so-called scientific exegesis hesitates to speak of Christ, nor does it see him practically in any passage of the Old Testament, or it is fearful to say that it sees him there, for fear of disqualifying "scientifically." The two excesses of hyper-criticism and fundamentalism are opposite only in appearance: as I have already said, they both have in common the fact of stopping at the letter and neglecting the Spirit.

The most serious problem of a certain exclusively scientific exegesis is that it completely changes the relationship between the scholar and the word of God. To understand what this statement means, one has to take into account what has happened in the general field of theology. We have by now good studies that reconstruct the evolution of the meaning of the word "theology" from its origin to our days. These studies show a very clear evolution and a sort of fracture that happened around the twelfth century. Up until this date, the term theology indicated "a certain way of knowing God and of speaking of him," a way filled with praise, adoration, and full acceptance of God in one's life.

Theology is mostly seen as a *wisdom*, as a grace and a charism. It was thought that only the Holy Spirit who searches the depth of God, can teach to speak of God. "If you are a theologian you will really pray, and if you really pray, you are a theologian," said Evagrius.[6] The first time in which the word "to theologize" (*theologein*) appears in Christian language, the meaning is that of "to proclaim with hymns the divinity of Christ."[7]

Starting in the twelfth century, theology acquires a new meaning: that of an organic and scholarly knowledge of the facts of revelation, a reasoned exposition of what pertains to Christian religion. In short, the notion of theology as science is born. At the time when this change was occurring, there was nothing especially revolutionary about it. It didn't exclude that religious component of humble submission to God, forever bound to the activity of theology, considered the queen of the sciences. In the universities, it was considered to be the highest ranking of all disciplines. It was theology, so to speak, that "informed" the other sciences, and all the sciences, on the other hand, were perceived in a sacred, religious tone.

The trouble was to reveal itself later on, when the relationships changed. The sciences became free, the topmost science became philosophy and finally, in the last centuries, physics and, today, biology. At this point, it's the other sciences that insensibly impose their status of science to theology. In fact, one of the postulates of science theory is that scientists remain neutral in front of their object of research; they must dominate and master it. When we wish to praise a scientist, we say, in fact, that he or she masters the object of his or her discipline perfectly.

But when this scientific principle, so very valid elsewhere, is applied to theology, it then appears aberrant. How can one "master" God or Scripture? Only in this case, the object is above the subject and cannot be mastered, one cannot remain neutral in front of it.

What Saint Paul says, in the letter to the Romans, about impiety sheds light also on this field of Scripture. We can say of Scripture what we say of creation: what we can know of God is revealed in it, manifested to humankind. So those who scrutinize Scripture without giving glory and thanks to the author are inexcusable, but they're delirious in their own thoughts and place creatures above the Creator; namely, they place their creature, their exegesis and hermeneutics, above the work of the creator, which is, precisely, Scripture (cf. Rom 1:18ff.).

What would we say of philologists who were to study the sources of Dante, their evolution, the state of the themes before these would be accepted by the author and transformed into the *Divine Comedy*, and were to end up considering this the most important and serious thing, much more than reading, appreciating and admiring, and letting oneself be taken by the delight of its poetry, the strength of the inspiration, and the final form taken by these materials? And what would we say of scholars who would consider reconstructing the various forms assumed by the legend of *Faust* from Marlowe to Goethe or the stages of evolution of the symphonic genre before Beethoven much more important than reading the work of *Faust* itself or listening to the Ninth Symphony? Or what if such scholars might even be afraid of being moved by the power of the two masterpieces, fearing to fail in their duty of critics? Yet this is what has been occurring now for a while in certain settings with the divinely inspired Scriptures. The most important task has become that of tearing them apart in order to reconstruct them.

The consequence of all this is the closing up and folding of Scripture upon itself; it goes back to being the "sealed" book, the "veiled" book because, says Saint Paul, "whenever a person turns to the Lord the veil is removed," meaning when one recognizes Christ in the pages of Scripture (cf. 2 Cor 3:15-16). In the Bible something similar happens to what occurs to certain extremely sensitive plants that close their leaves when touched by foreign objects; certain shells also close their valves to protect the pearl within. The pearl of Scripture is Christ.

It's difficult to explain otherwise the many crises of faith of biblical scholars. When it's asked why certain seminaries and places of formation suffer from such spiritual poverty and aridity, one is quick to learn that one of the main causes is the way Scripture is taught there. The Church has lived and lives from a spiritual reading of the Bible; once this path that nourishes the life of piety is cut off, zeal and faith dry up and languish. The liturgy, completely built on the spiritual use of the Bible, is no longer understood; or it is lived as a moment detached from a real, personal formation and contradicted from what had been learned the previous day in class.

3. The Spirit Gives Life

When we spend quite some time without using a part of the body, for instance, a foot, we have, then, to exercise and reeducate the limb if we want to walk again. Christians need to be reeducated in the use of the Bible. For some, this retraining consists in starting to pick up a Bible and read it, because maybe they haven't yet seriously approached it in its entirety. For others who know it and have even studied it at length, reeducation consists in getting reacquainted with that spiritual reading of Scripture, which, during the whole patristic and medieval period, was the primary source of the wisdom and spirituality of the Church.

A sign of great hope is that some prominent scholars are now beginning to notice the need for a spiritual and faith-based reading of Scripture. One of them recently wrote: "It's urgent for those who study and interpret Scripture that they foster a renewed interest in the exegesis of the fathers, to re-discover, beyond their methods, the soul that animated them, the deep spirit that inspired their exegesis. We must learn to interpret Scripture at their school, not only from the historical and critical point of view, but also in the Church and for the Church" (I. de la Potterie). In a justly famous work on medieval exegesis, Fr. Henri de Lubac has brought to light the coherence, solidity, and extraordinary fecundity of the spiritual exegesis practiced by the ancient and medieval fathers.

But it must be said that in this field, the fathers only applied (with the imperfect instruments at their disposal) the pure and simple teaching of the New Testament; in other words, they aren't the initiators but those who continue a tradition that had, among its founders, John, Paul, and Jesus himself. They not only practiced a spiritual reading of the Scriptures—that is, a reading referenced in Christ—but also justified such a reading, declaring that all of Scripture speaks of Christ (cf. John 5:39), that contained in it was already "the spirit of Christ" operating and expressed through the prophets (cf. 1 Pet 1:11), that everything in the Old Testament is said "via allegory," namely, in reference to the Church (cf. Gal 4:24) or "as a warning to us" (1 Cor 10:11).

A spiritual reading of the Bible doesn't mean an edifying, mystical, subjective, or, even worse, a fanciful reading as opposed to a scientific reading that instead would be objective. On the contrary, it's the most objective reading there is because it is based on the Spirit of God, not on the spirit of man. The subjective reading of Scripture (based on free examination of the text) prevailed precisely when the spiritual reading was abandoned and where this took place, particularly in the Protestant theology.

A spiritual reading is something much more objective because it is the reading made under the guidance, or in the light of, the Holy Spirit that inspired the Scriptures. It is based on a historical event, on the redemptive act of Christ who, with his death and resurrection, fulfills the plan of salvation, realizes all the figures and prophecies, unveils all the hidden mysteries, and offers the real key to the reading of the whole Bible. Revelation expresses all this with the image of the sacrificed Lamb that takes the book into its hands and breaks the seven seals (cf. Rev 5:1ff.).

Anyone who would continue to read Scripture irrespective of this act, would be similar to a person reading a musical score in the key of G, after the composer has introduced the piece in the key of F. At that point, every single note would emit a false and discordant sound. Now, the New Testament calls the new key "the Spirit," while it defines the old key "the letter," saying that the letter brings death, but the Spirit gives life (2 Cor 3:6).

To compare "the letter" and "the Spirit" does not mean to contrast the Old and the New Testament, as if the first represented only the letter and the second only the Spirit. It means rather to contrast two different ways of reading both the Old and the New Testament, one way that places Christ aside and another way, instead, that judges everything in the light of Christ. Therefore, the Church can value both testaments, because both speak to it of Christ.

The spiritual way of reading gives to the Old Testament a new strength and suggestion unknown earlier, born only in the moment when we discover that it's speaking of something else. Beyond having a concrete and literal meaning, it also has a symbolic one that pushes beyond its own limits; in more traditional words, in the moment in which it's discovered, it speaks, by "allegory" (Gal 4:24).

Saint Augustine wrote:

> Anything that is suggested by means of symbols strikes and kindles our affections much more forcefully than the truth itself would do if presented unadorned with mysterious symbols. . . . Our sensibility is less easily kindled when still involved in purely concrete realities, but if it is first turned towards symbols drawn from the corporeal world, and thence again to the plane of those spiritual realities signified by those symbols, it gathers strength by the mere act of passing from one to the other and, like the flame of a burning torch, is made by the motion to burn all the brighter.[8]

For the Christian, something similar happens in the passage from the Old to the New Testament, from prophecy to reality. In this passage, the mind "is inflamed" like a moving torch. The description of the sufferings of the ailing servant in Isaiah 53, has a special way of speaking to us of the passion of Christ that no other historical narration in the gospels can replace. The indirect language, both the symbolic one of the sacraments and the prophetic one of Scripture, is less prone, in a certain sense, to extinction because it says but doesn't say. More than affirm, it suggests every time it recalls to the mind and provokes a new movement of the heart. The Old Testament therefore is not devalued by spiritual reading; on the contrary, it's exalted to the maximum. When Saint Paul says, the Spirit gives life, we must infer that it also gives life to the letter, even to the Old Testament!

4. What the Spirit Says to the Church

Spiritual reading, however, pertains not only to the Old Testament but to the New Testament as well. To read the

New Testament spiritually means to read it in light of the Holy Spirit given at Pentecost to the Church in order to lead it to the whole truth, namely, to the full comprehension and realization of the Gospel.

Jesus himself explained, in advance, the relationship between his word and the Spirit that he would send (we must not think that he necessarily did so in the precise terms used in this regard in the Gospel of John). We read in John: "[H]e will teach you everything and remind you of all that [I] told you" (John 14:25-26), namely, he will make it understood in depth, in all its implications. He "will not speak on his own," namely, he will not say new things related to what Jesus said but, as Jesus himself says, "he will take from what is mine and declare it to you" (John 16:13-15).

Jesus did not say everything openly; there were things of which the disciples were not yet able to "carry the weight"; the Holy Spirit is in charge of leading the disciples to the fullness of the truth not yet attained. We can therefore say that spiritual reading, in its full and comprehensive sense, is one in which the Holy Spirit teaches us to read the New Testament in reference to Jesus and to read the Old and the New Testament together in reference to the Church.

We can see in this how spiritual reading integrates and surpasses scientific reading, which knows only one direction, that of history; it explains, in fact, what comes after in light of what comes before. It explains the New Testament in light of the Old that precedes it and explains the Church in light of the New Testament. A good portion of the critical effort around Scripture consists in illustrating the doctrine of the gospel in the light of Old Testament traditions and of rabbinical exegesis. It consists, in short, of the inquiry of the sources (and on this principle the Kittel and many other biblical aids are based).

Spiritual reading fully recognizes the validity of this direction in research but adds to it an opposite one. It consists in explaining what comes before in the light of what comes after, prophecy in the light of realization, the Old Testament in the light of the New Testament, and the New Testament in the light of the tradition of the Church. Only after the realization of God's plan can we fully understand the meaning of what prepared and prefigured it. Here, the spiritual reading of the Bible finds unusual confirmation in the hermeneutic principle of Gadamer of the "history of the effects" (*Wirkungsgeschichte*). According to this theory, in order to understand a text, one must take into account the effects it has produced in history, entering into this history and carrying on a dialogue with it.[9]

This—as I mentioned earlier—is not only valid for the passage from the Old to the New Testament, but also for the passage from the New Testament to the Church, because only in the light of what the Holy Spirit accomplishes in the Church do we discover the infinite possibilities and implications of the word and of the mystery of Christ. Tradition is similar to a large echo chamber of Scripture. What would a violin be in which only the cords were to vibrate, without that marvelous cavity, made of a select, seasoned, and planed wood, in which the sound takes shape? What would the Song of Songs be, if read simply as it lies within the biblical codes, without that resonance it has had in the liturgy and the spirituality of the Church, applied either to the Church itself, or to Mary, or to the soul enamored of God?

If, as Jesus says, every tree is recognized by its fruits, the word of God also cannot be fully known, before having seen the fruit it has produced. To study Scripture in the light of Tradition is a bit like knowing the tree from its fruit. This is why Origen said that "the spiritual sense is the one the Spirit gives to the Church."[10] It's identified with ecclesiastical reading or even Tradition itself, if by Tradition we mean not only the solemn declarations of the magisterium (that concern, actually, very few biblical texts) but also the experience of doctrine and sanctity in which the word of God has newly been incarnated and "explained" over the course of centuries through the work of the Holy Spirit.

What is happening then, is not a spiritual reading that takes the place of current scientific exegesis, with an automatic return to the exegesis of the fathers. It is rather a new spiritual reading that corresponds to the enormous progress brought on by the study of the "letter." In a word, a reading that has the breath and faith of the fathers and at the same time the consistency and seriousness of current biblical science.

5. The Spirit that Blows from All Corners

Facing an expanse of dried bones, the prophet Ezekiel heard this question: "[C]an these bones come to life?" (Ezek 37:3). Today, we ask ourselves the same question: will exegesis, parched by the long excesses of philology, be able to recapture the impetus and life that it had at other moments in the history of the people of God? Father de Lubac, after studying the long history of Christian exegesis, concludes rather dismally, saying that "we contemporaries lack the conditions favorable to reviving a spiritual reading like that of the fathers; we're lacking that faith full of enthusiasm, that sense of fullness and unity that they had, so that attempting today to imitate their audacity would almost expose us to a kind of profanation, since we lack the spirit out of which things originated then."[11] Yet he doesn't totally close the door on hope and claims that "if we want to rediscover something of what was, in the first centuries of the Church, the spiritual interpretation of the Scriptures, we must first of all recreate a spiritual movement."[12]

A few decades later, interspersed with Vatican Council II, I seem to detect in these last words, a prophecy. That "spiritual movement" and that "impetus" have begun to resurface, not because humankind planned or foresaw them, but because the Spirit started unexpectedly to breathe again from all corners on the dry bones. Contemporaneously with the reappearance of the charisma, we're also seeing the reappearance of the spiritual reading of the Bible, and this too is one of the most delectable fruits of the Spirit.

Whenever I participate in biblical and prayer encounters, I'm surprised to hear at times, reflections on the word of God completely similar to those made in their time by Origen, Augustine, or Gregory the Great, even if in simpler language. The words on the temple, on the "tent of David," on Jerusalem destroyed and rebuilt after the exile, are applied, very simply and pertinently, to the Church, to Mary, to one's own community or personal life. What is narrated about the characters of the Old Testament, makes us think (by analogy or antithesis) of Jesus and what is narrated about Jesus is applied and realized in reference to the Church and the individual believer.

What causes many perplexities regarding the spiritual reading of the Bible is that there is little consideration of the distinction between explanation and application. In spiritual reading, more than claiming to explain the text, giving to it a meaning extraneous to the intention of the sacred author, in general it's a matter of giving life to the text. And we see this happening already in the New Testament regarding the words of Jesus. We notice at times that, of the same parable of Jesus, different applications are made in the Synoptics according to the needs and problems of the community for which each one is writing.

The applications of the fathers and those of today do not evidently have the canonical character of these original applications. But the process that leads to them is the same and based on the fact that the words of God are not dead words, "to be preserved in oil," as Peguy would say; they are "live" and "active" words, able to emit hidden meanings and possibilities, in response to new questions and situations. This is the result of what I called the "active inspiration" of Scriptures, of the fact that they are not only "inspired by the Holy Spirit" but also "breathing forth" the Spirit if read with faith. Gregory the Great said, "Scripture—*cum legentibus crescit*—grows with those who read it."[13] It grows, while remaining intact.

I will end with a prayer that I heard a woman say, after the reading of the story of Elijah who, ascending to heaven, leaves in Elysium two thirds of his spirit. This is an example of spiritual reading in the sense I've just explained. "Thank you, Jesus, for going to heaven and not leaving us only two thirds of your Spirit, but your full Spirit! And thank you for not leaving it to only one disciple, but to all humankind."

Notes

Chapter I

1. W. Goethe, *Faust*, Part 1.
2. J. P. Sartre, *No Exit and Three Other Plays* (Vintage International, New York, 1989), p. 45.
3. *Le piu' belle preghiere del mondo* (edited by V. Cattana, Mondadori, Milano, 2000), p. 188.

Chapter II

1. Cf. Augustine, *Letters*, 55, 1, 2.
2. *Sacrosanctum Concilium* 7.
3. *Dei Verbum* 8.
4. St. John of the Cross, *Ascent of Mount Carmel*, 2.22.4-5.
5. Cf. *Lumen Gentium* 48.
6. Augustine, *Treatise on the Gospel of John*, 80, 3.
7. J. B. Bossuet, *Oeuvres Oratoires de Bossuet, III* (Desclee de Brouwer, Paris, 1927), p. 627.
8. Augustine, *Confessions*, VIII, 12.
9. Origen, *In Exodum homilia* 13, 3 (PG 12,391).
10. *Regole monastiche d'occidente* (Quiqajon, Communita' di Bose, 1989), p. 53.

Chapter III

1. E. P. Sanders, *Jesus and Judaism* (London, 1985).
2. J. Neusner, *A Rabbi Talks with Jesus* (McGill–Queen's University Press, Montreal, 2000).
3. Irenaeus, *Adv.Haer.*, IV, 34,1.
4. J. Neusner, op. cit., p. 84.
5. Cf. J. D. G. Dunn, *Christianity in the Making, I. Jesus remembered* (Grand Rapids, Mich, 2003).
6. Benedict XVI, *Gesu' di Nazaret* (Rizzoli, Milano, 2007), p. 10.
7. R. Dawkins, *God Delusion* (Bantam Books, 2006).

8. On the theory of Jesus as a cynic, cf. B. Griffin, *Was Jesus a Philosophical Cynic?* [http://www.oxford.op.org/allen/html/acts/htm].

9. Cf. the essay by Harold Bloom, *Whoever Discovers the Interpretation of These Sayings. . .* published as an appendix to an edition of the Coptic Gospel of Thomas edited by Marvin Meyer, *The Gospel of Thomas: The Hidden Sayings of Jesus* (Harper Collins, San Francisco, 1992).

10. W. Bossuet, *Kyrios Christos* (Vandenhoeck & Ruprecht, Goettinger, 1913).

11. L. Hurtado, *Lord Jesus Christ. Devotion to Jesus in Earliest Christianity* (Grand Rapids, Mich. 2003), p. 650.

12. Cf. J. D. G. Dunn, op. cit., part III, ch12.

13. *Insegnamenti di Paolo VI*, vol X, Tipografia Poliglotta Vaticana, p. 1210 s. (Discourse of 29 Nov. 1972); translation in E. O'Connor, *Pope Paul and the Spirit*, Ave Maria Press, Notre Dame, Indiana 1978, p.183).

Chapter IV

1. S. Kierkegaard, *Fear and Trembling* ("Panegyric upon Abraham"), trans. by W. Lowrie (Princeton: Princeton University Press, 1954), p. 30.

Chapter V

1. Cf. M. Zerwick, *Analysis philologica Novi Testamenti Graeci* (Rome, 1953).

2. C. Peguy, *"Le porche du mystere de la deuxieme vertu"* in *Oeuvres Poetiques completes* (Gallimard, Paris, 1975), p. 587.

3. Cf. Origen, *In Mt Ser., 38* (GCS, 1925, p. 202).

4. J. B. Bossuet, *Sur la parole de Dieu*, in *Oeuvres oratoires de Bossuet* III (Desclee de Brouwer, Paris, 1927), p. 628.

Chapter VI

1. St. Ambrose, *Exp. Ps.*, 118, 7, 7.

2. *Dei Verbum* 21.

3. John Paul II, *Novo millennio ineunte*, n. 39.

4. Benedict XVI, in AAS 97, 2005, p. 957.

5. *Dei Verbum* 25.

6. S. Kierkegaard, *For Self-examination* (OUP, 1946), p. 64S.

7. F. Collins, *The Language of God* (Free Press, New York, 2006), p. 177.

8. Guigo II, *The Ladder of Monks* (Oxford, 1978), pp. 81–95.

9. St. Augustine, *Enarr. In Ps., 46, 1* (CCL 38, 529).

10. St. Gregory the Great, *Registri Epistolarum* 4, 31 (PL 77, 706).

11. St. Augustine, *De catechizandis rudibus* 1.8 (PL 40, 319).

12. St. Augustine, *Soliloquies* 2.1 (PL 32, 885).

13. Origen, *In Gen .Hom.*, 12, 5.

14. Celano, *Vita Secunda*, X, 15 (FF 601).

15. St. Augustine, *Confessions*, 8, 12.

16. St. Theresa of Lisieux, *Manuscript A*, 236.

17. St. Gregory the Great, *On Ezekiel*, 1, 10, 31 (CCL 142, p.159).

18. St. Augustine, *Confessions*, XI, 2, 3-4.

Chapter VII

1. Henri de Lubac, *Exegese medievale*, 1, 1 (Paris, 1964), p. 79.

2. St. Ambrose, *De Spiritu Sancto*, III, 112.

3. St. Augustine, *Confessions*, IV, 12, 18.

4. *Dei Verbum* 21.

5. S. Kierkagaard, *For Self-examination*, 58.

6. Evagrius Ponticus, *De Oratione*, 60 (PG 79, 1180).

7. Cf. Eusebius of Cesarea, *Church History*, V, 28, 5.

8. St. Augustine, *Ep. 55*, 11, 21.

9. Cf. H. G. Gadamer, *Wahrheit und Methode* (Tubingen, 1960).

10. Origen, *In Leviticum Homilia* 5.5 (PG 12, 454).

11. Henri de Lubac, op. cit., II, 2.

12. Henri de Lubac, *Histoire et Esprit* (Paris, 1950) (Conclusion).

13. St. Gregory the Great, *Commentary on Job*, 20, 1 (CC 143A, p. 1003).